MALARIA MEMOIRS

My Life Journey as a
Public Health Doctor in Tanzania

Zul Premji

MAWENZI
HOUSE

Published with the generous assistance of the Canada Council for the Arts and the Ontario Arts Council. We also acknowledge the support of the Government of Canada through the Canada Book Fund and the Government of Ontario through the Ontario Book Publishing Tax Credit.

Cover design by Sabrina Pignataro
Cover image: aleksandarvelasevic / Hand Drawn Circles Background stock illustration / iStockphoto

Library and Archives Canada Cataloguing in Publication

Title: Malaria memoirs : my life journey as a public health doctor in Tanzania / Zul Premji.
Names: Premji, Zul, author.
Identifiers: Canadiana (print) 20210191171 | Canadiana (ebook) 20210191554 | ISBN 9781774150351
   (softcover) | ISBN 9781774150368 (EPUB) | ISBN 9781774150375 (PDF)
Subjects: LCSH: Premji, Zul. | LCSH: Physicians—Tanzania—Biography. | LCSH: Malaria—Tanzania—
   History. | LCSH: Public health—Tanzania—History. | LCGFT: Autobiographies.
Classification: LCC R654.P74 A3 2021 | DDC 610.92—dc23

Printed and bound in Canada by Coach House Printing

Mawenzi House Publishers Ltd.
39 Woburn Avenue (B)
Toronto, Ontario M5M 1K5
Canada

www.mawenzihouse.com

To

Zeenat, Zainil, Zaaher, and Zarrin, and Reeshma
whom I think of affectionately as "$Z^4 + 1$"

Contents

Foreword

The unexamined life is not worth living.

SOCRATES

All my working life I have been a simple malariologist. I was never a celebrity nor was I ever a high-ranking politician, so why should anybody read my story? Writing one's memoir is in a sense blowing one's own trumpet. It is prone to vanity and inaccuracy, even dishonesty. Can it or its motivation be trusted? I have given this a long thought and in the end decided to go ahead, promising myself to be as balanced as possible.

My working life was involved with the well-known, terrible, and controversial disease of malaria. It is controversial because to my mind it is a political, social, and economic disease of a society as well as a pathology of the human body that uses medical science in its diagnosis and treatment. There is a very strong public health component in its diagnosis and treatment that had a major influence on my life.

This is a story of seemingly impossible quests and grand objectives. It reflects the importance of the hard work, honesty, and integrity that are required in medical research. At its heart is the sheer excitement of science and the satisfaction obtained in successful treatment and saving a child's life. I went from a destitute childhood in a village, with little prospect in sight, to become by persistence and luck a medical laboratory technician—which would have satisfied most people—and go on to become a doctor and a professor of pathology who was able to save the lives of poor children. It is this journey, coupled with my personal life, that I intend to trace in this book.

I would like the human factor in the practice of medicine, especially in a poor country like Tanzania, to emerge here. I have seen that the power of the human spirit can be stronger than any drug or vaccine.

All my working life I worked at a public medical school. I grew up when a socialist ideology was in force in Tanzania, therefore perhaps my thinking is skewed towards how public health should benefit the masses. Post retirement I worked as professor of pathology at a private medical university for three years, hence in what follows I also cover my experiences of the lesser satisfaction I had there.

Memoirs are written to help make sense of our lives; it is all too human to dwell on our mistakes, our triumphs, and those electrical moments when a life-changing decision is made. This is one such attempt.

1

My Early Years

The best way to predict your future is to create it.

ABRAHAM LINCOLN

Some sixty-seven years ago I was accidentally born in the small historical town of Iringa, now a sizable city in Tanzania. Iringa is situated on the globe at the latitude of 7.77°S and longitude of 35.69°E. The name is derived from the KiHehe word *lilinga*, meaning "fort." KiHehe is the language of the Hehe people. The Hehe strongly resisted German colonization of the region in the early twentieth century, and there is a popular legend about how their leader, Chief Mkwawa, never gave up until his death.

I say I was born accidently in Iringa because my family was travelling at the time, passing through Iringa when I decided to end fetal life. I never actually saw Iringa until around 1990 when I visited it for the first time. It's one of the cleanest cities in Tanzania and the climate is ideally temperate just as in Nairobi.

I was the last born in a family of six siblings. We were four brothers and two sisters, an optimum family size at that time, though in current times it would be considered large. My early years were spent in Morogoro, a town about a hundred miles west of the commercial capital, Dar es Salaam. We were there until I was eleven.

My parents were not educated, and I was brought up in the midst of poverty, and it was fairly common for us to have one meal a day. This was not of much concern to me because in our neighbourhood there were many mango trees and I could easily pluck a few unripe or ripe mangoes. These would fill the void of a missed meal. There were not only mangoes but other tropical fruits as well, like papaya, zambarau (black plum), mapera (guava), and kungu (Indian almond fruit).

We had a small shop about an hour's walk from the centre of Morogoro, in an area known as Nungwe and the nearby neighbourhood was Mji Mpya. Ours was the only Asian or Indian-origin family in the African area. Our shop could be described in the local terminology as a pilipili-bizari shop (literally meaning red curry powder and turmeric, half a teaspoon, expertly wrapped in a slip of a newspaper). Other items were cigarette sticks (one could even buy half a stick!), kerosene, rice, maize flour and similar basic items that one needs. The total inventory would be worth perhaps two or three hundred dollars. This popular duka (shop) would not be even one tenth of what a Seven Eleven outlet would be.

After a few years the shop would collapse, and we would have to relocate to another area or to another town. In 1963 we relocated to Tanga, a coastal town after my dad was imprisoned. I recall in Morogoro before the shop my dad was employed as a caretaker (jamat bhai) of our Ismaili mosque (jamatkhana). I am not sure about the reason why he quit, but I faintly remember family discussions pertaining to some non-payments of bonuses. When the 48th Ismaili Imam passed away, in his will all such employees of the mosques were to be paid a modest sum of money.

But despite our poverty, what I recall is a fairly happy childhood, unstructured and with absolute freedom. Most of the daytime was spent outdoors. Children of the neighbourhood (Africans except myself and my older brother) would get together and play soccer, using a ball often made out of rags. We would be outdoors until sunset, only going home or to a friend's house to alleviate hunger pangs.

In Morogoro, I started going to what I understand was a nursery school, where we had a strict, elderly teacher who amazingly seemed to know everything. She was our sole teacher. We played a lot and learned a few things but I always thought other kids knew far too much more than I did. Maybe they were tutored at home by their parents or elder siblings. No one had taught me numbers, how to add and subtract single digits, and the alphabet, which these kids seemed equipped with.

There was one life event that has lingered in my mind; it was why my family relocated from Morogoro to Tanga. In January 1963, when I was ten, my father was jailed in Morogoro for one month and seven days for his inability to pay a debt of 500 shillings (equal to about seventy American dollars at the time). I vividly remember the difficulty my mom had to face. The Ismaili community was very strong, and we have an unwritten tradition to help each other, especially when a debtor was from the same community. I remember the debtor as Dakawa Traders, but even today I fail to understand why he took such a drastic step as to get my father imprisoned. This was the sad part of my last days in Morogoro. Even today, whenever I visit Morogoro, this painful episode comes back to haunt me. I wish I had been a little older and helped out at the time. I am pretty sure that such an incident cannot take place today, because the community has developed and put into place structures for arbitration and conflict resolution boards in every region where they reside. That was not the case in the sixties, though there were local leaders who perhaps could have intervened but did not, and I do not know why.

This was my first real encounter with the popular saying that it is expensive to be poor.

My elder sister, Gulshan, was our third born and ten years older than me. Today I know that she had what is known as acne vulgaris. This skin condition, mostly involving the face, has a deep psychological impact on teenagers. I recall that she loved me dearly, was kind and helpful, always shared snacks with me and played with me. I never had any store-bought toys to play with, but we made our own toys—balls and dolls made of rags, and cars made with peeled bamboo stalks for their bodies and thread reels for wheels. One day in Morogoro she took me to Metropolitan Cinema to watch my first Hindi film, *Dil Deke Dekho*, which was a hit in 1959 with a popular star cast including Shammi Kapoor and Asha Parekh. I had to sit on her lap for the entire two and a half hours that the film lasted.

I felt very sad when my father decided that she should get married at the age of twenty, she could not continue with her education. After marriage she joined her husband in a small village near Morogoro known as Matombo, where they had a small convenience shop. I had the opportunity to visit her for a few days when I became severely sick, with a high temperature and shivers typical of malaria episodes. I think I was treated with Paludrine tablets (now I know its clinical name to be proguanil), and she nursed me, applying onions all over my body to reduce the fever. Throughout my life and even as I write this I have remained close to her; she is in her late seventies residing in Toronto with her elder daughter. Fortunately I am able to talk with her on WhatsApp. I consider her as my mother and had she continued with her education she would have had, I suppose, a much happier life. She has three daughters and one son. I remember that she lost her second son in Tanzania in 1966 due to enteric fever and dehydration. Apart from this one tragic event she has led a fulfilling married life.

Apart from the above, what I remember most from my childhood in Morogoro were the sounds, the smells, the colourful chaos, and the daily contradictions. I knew all the streets and alleys of Morogoro and I had friends there. I am not sure whether I was thrilled by the news of our abrupt relocation, the idea of plunging into the colourful dynamics of a relatively bigger town, or was daunted by the prospect of change and not knowing what to expect. This was my sadness and dilemma about the move to Tanga. There were so many things happening around me—packing all our possessions and rushing around for last-minute purchases—but no one would tell me more about why we were moving, what Tanga would be like. With all these uncertainties and questions on my mind, it was indeed an upheaval that I went through.

With these doubts, a nervous ten-year-old boy moved from Morogoro to Tanga by bus on the rough roads as they were then and saw the Indian Ocean for the first time, wondering how people could stay afloat in water without sinking.

My fear was about being alone, without friends. I had been told that there would be many more people around, but everyone would be wrapped up in their own worlds and pay me no attention at all. I would feel lonely and isolated even amidst a big crowd. But this move to a bigger town taught me a number of valuable lessons. I would learn to find solutions when there seemed to be no solution at all; to stand up for my beliefs and assert myself; to look at my life with new perspectives and heightened awareness. The competitive nature of the big town provoked me to look for constant improvement and self-development, to achieve the best in anything I did. I learned to welcome challenges and not to be held back by fears and doubts. I would learn to shape my own life.

2

Life in Tanga

Success consists of going from failure to failure without loss of enthusiasm.

WINSTON CHURCHILL

I remember only faintly the bus journey from Morogoro to Tanga. In those days the road was dirt and in rainy weather impassable. We went via the town of Handeni and it was about a fourteen-hour bumpy ride. We were now six in the family, four brothers and our parents. I missed my sister Gulshan. At the time, compared to Morogoro, Tanga was a bustling town on the coast of the Indian Ocean near the border with Kenya. This was the first time I saw the ocean. In a few days I started to discover the fine clean beaches majestically lined with coconut trees. There were two swimming clubs, an expensive one mostly patronized by Europeans (ie, whites) and another by Africans and Asians. I learned how to swim in Tanga at the ocean by just starting to play in the warm water.

The first few weeks in Tanga were terrible for us; we had little food and the six of us lived in a small room at the corner of Barabara Nane (Eighth Street) and Miti Ulaya Street. My dad was a tall and hefty, confident person; his philosophy of life was a blend of common sense and practical wisdom, and recognizing that you know what you know and are ignorant of what you don't know. With his children he was strict, no-nonsense and authoritarian, but in his own way he was loving and made us imbibe the art of being honest. According to him determination and persistence are indispensable in life.

On the other hand my mom was soft spoken and caring, always there for us, listening and protecting us; her expressions spoke more than anything else. From her I learned that despite the harsh reality of our poverty-stricken life, we had to be simple and realistic. One thing she would say is, "Ice and embers cannot lie in the same bowl."

Soon after our arrival in Tanga, my father started making the Indian sweet, known as jugu paak, to sell. This sweet, shaped into a parallelogram, was made from roasted peanuts, sugar, jaggery, and water. The cooking was highly labour-intensive and took place mostly at night time, the final baking being done in red-hot clay ovens. The jugu paaks were sold to a number of small shops in Tanga. Initially my dad himself would deliver them to each shop, but with time he bought a bicycle, which had a unique colourful metal attachment to carry the heavy load. This conspicuous bicycle was a good marketing tool.

Since there was no other option, we continued to invest our energy in this small business. With time we were able to move to a bigger house and also opened a small retail shop, a sort of convenience store. The credit for this initial small success goes to my elder brother Aziz, the fifth born, who was about fifteen at the time. He helped my father with the cooking and gradually learned how to make the jugu paaks in bulk. I recall days when we were all involved in the process, because of high demand.

I started primary school in grade five at Tayabali Sachak Primary

School—TSPS—in the Bombo area. For the first time I saw a big primary school. It had about 800 pupils, there were one to eight streams and each stream had two classes. There were about forty pupils in each class. Despite the high number, the quality of education was of a very high standard. TSPS was mostly for the benefit of children from the Bohra community, and there were very few non-Bohra kids there. The rich families of the Bohra community through donations had built a whole education complex, consisting of a primary school, a secondary school, hostels, and sports facilities, so that their children from all over Tanzania could study at TSPS.

It was an excellent school and very well managed, and today there are many professionals like doctors, engineers, high court judges, and accountants who have passed through it and contributed towards the development of Tanzania. Here, I was for the first time exposed to learning the holy Quran in Arabic. This was totally rote learning—loudly reciting the verses from the Book—and to me it presented a battle between memorization and using intelligence. The worst part of this practice was the punishment meted out for the slightest mistake or at times for even no mistake. The teachers walked around with a plaited electrical wire (one particular cane was nicknamed Madagascar), which was lashed with full force. In present times this would be considered serious child abuse; I was its recipient a number of times because I was a perpetual absconder from these classes. I do believe in the holy Quran, but not in rote learning and corporal punishment. We Ismailis are not forced but encouraged to learn the holy Quran. I read the English version when I was about twenty years old.

The leader of the Bohras is known as His Holiness, who at about the time we arrived in Tanga in 1963 was their 50th leader. He lived in India. Tanga had a large Bohra presence. His Holiness came to TSPS during his visit to Tanga, and the pupils were allowed an audience with him. We were instructed carefully about the procedures to follow. Three pupils at a time would approach him very respectfully where he was seated, kiss his hands and feet and walk backwards out of his presence, without showing him their backs. All this was completely fine with me and I was accompanied by a Somali pupil whose name was Abdillahi (I forget the name of the other boy), and together we approached him wearing traditional Islamic caps. His Holiness appeared to be a simple, sweet, and very humble wise man, who spoke in a low tone and mostly listened. I vividly remember him asking me about my faith, and I replied that I was an Ismaili. He was very happy with that and directed me to give one shilling and twenty-five cents to the Ismaili jamatkhana (prayer house). An offering of one shilling and twenty-five cents is a symbolic gesture made to alleviate one's problems. I was amazed by His Holiness's knowledge about this small tradition. What I did not do that day was to kiss his hands and feet, because in my faith we never do that even to our own leader, His Highness the Aga Khan.

The teachers took this as very disrespectful, and we were punished by the head teacher, who was a South Indian, Mr Narayan. By sheer coincidence, many years later, in 1989, I was the one called upon to certify his death as an emergency doctor at the Aga Khan Hospital in Dar es Salaam.

My one-year stay at TSPS ended and I was accepted to join class six at the Aga Khan Primary School (AKPS) for the year 1964. I think my parents sought this relocation because they wanted me to learn the concept and practices of our own faith, which were taught at AKPS.

I felt more comfortable at the Aga Khan school, which was smaller with fewer students because the Ismaili community was smaller in Tanga. This school was closer to my home, so that despite the hot sun I was able to walk to school. I need to share an important event that changed the course of my life. Academically I was a poor performer. My marks were well below average, because I lacked an understanding of some basic concepts. I failed miserably in the class six final examination and therefore was directed to repeat the year. I was devastated because my classmates had started class seven while I had to repeat class six. I cried and refused to go to school. But there was no alternative and finally I agreed under duress to repeat class six.

Fortunately we had a different class teacher, Mrs Helbling, an expatriate from California. She was very kind and her teaching was excellent. She made sure that everybody understood the lessons. She knew that I was a repeater and took extra efforts to make sure I understood. Once she told me a German proverb: *"Could everything be done twice, everything would be done better."* She insisted that I do the best I could and so it was. I ranked first in the final examination. I remember her even to this day, though I have no knowledge of where she is. By simple arithmetic, if she was thirty years of age in 1965, she should be eighty-five years old in 2020. I hope she is in good health and enjoying her life, but if she has gone from this world, may her soul rest in peace.

Back to class seven at AKPS. I was selected to be the head boy of the school. This was my first leadership position and it also shaped my future by preparing me for the leadership positions I would hold in my working life. We had a new headmaster, Mr Kapasi, who was very strict and did not hesitate to impart physical punishment; caning was fairly common even for a trivial misconduct like being late by a few minutes. I was totally opposed to such harsh punishment, thus as head boy I never took any student to the headmaster for a misbehaviour; instead I would take time and explain to students what they had done wrong. Perhaps in the process I may have created a few chronic recalcitrants but I believe that the majority of the students perceived my attitude positively and not as a weakness.

In the final days of class seven I had the opportunity to discuss my position with Mr Kapasi, but he stood his ground: "*Spare the rod and spoil the child.*"

Unfortunately my parents' objective in relocating me from TSPS to AKPS was not achieved. Because I hated any sort of physical punishment, I refused to attend religion classes. We had a new lady teacher for religion classes who also taught Gujarati. Once, due to some trivial issue, she prepared to punish me with a wooden ruler. Her method was to beat on the hand, palm downwards, with a pencil under the middle finger. I refused to take this and never attended the religion class again. I regret having missed the opportunity to learn Gujarati, though I never made any effort to learn our ancestral language again.

Another worthy incident took place in October that year. I was the head boy of the AKPS and the head girl was Naaz Teja. His Highness the Aga Khan, the Ismaili Imam, was visiting Tanga for a day. His visit is a very major event for his followers. He arrived in town that morning and his first stop was the AKPS to meet with teachers and pupils. Preparations had been made weeks before. As head boy and head girl, we were selected by Mr Kapasi to welcome the Imam. This entailed opening the car door and presenting a bouquet.

At the last minute we were told that we should be in the meeting hall and some local Ismaili council leader would do the welcoming. To date I cannot comprehend the reason for this abrupt change. I ask myself, was this perhaps because of my family's poverty? Had my family been rich and influential, would there have been a change in the program? I vividly recall Mr Kapasi's helpless expression when he directed me and Naaz to the meeting hall. Mr Kapasi was not an Ismaili and perhaps did not understand the undercurrents. Despite initial economic progress that we made as a family, we were not able to divorce ourselves from poverty. The end of 1966 saw another relocation. We moved from Tanga to Mtwara, which is the southernmost port of Tanzania. The incentive was that a philanthropist from the community had announced that he was seeking ten poor families to relocate to Mtwara; he would give to each family merchandise worth 10,000 shillings to help run a small shop. The caveat was that the shop had to be in the rural areas outside Mtwara town. My father seized this opportunity and in early November 1966 we went by bus to Mtwara.

In Tanzania in 1965 there was a major shift in education policy. The Ministry of Education limited primary school years to seven instead of eight. So in 1965 classes seven and eight took the same national "territorial examination" for qualifying to secondary schools at Form I. Many of my former classmates failed to qualify and had to seek entry to the newly opened private secondary school which is still there and known as Popatlal Secondary School. My repeating the year in class six was a blessing, because the following year there was no class eight. I passed the territorial qualifying examination in 1966 with flying colours and was selected for Form I in Karimjee Secondary School (now renamed Usagara Secondary School). This was a public school and provided free quality education. (Sometime in 1999 I took my son who was twenty-one years old to visit this school in Tanga; it was dilapidated and the quality of education had definitely declined. I was at a loss to explain to my son that this was once my secondary school.)

It was when we had just arrived in Mtwara that the territorial examinations results were announced and I was informed that I had been selected to join Karimjee Secondary School. And so my parents made arrangements for me to return to Tanga and stay there as a paying guest. This was done and I continued my studies in Form I. There were six classes in Form I, A to F, and I was in class E. Our class teacher was Mr Brampath, an older man with a lot of wisdom, and he taught us math. Some classes were taught traditional mathematics while other classes had a new curriculum; perhaps this was a pilot project for the new math curriculum.

I stayed with an Ismaili family that had migrated from Zanzibar after the revolution. Life was very good, the family was kind and treated me well but I missed my parents—this was the first time I had been separated from them. But I did well in my studies and was active in sports, playing soccer, cricket, and volleyball. This comfortable and rather stable life came to an abrupt end in August 1968, when I was in Form II. I received a telegram saying that my dad had been hospitalized due to a heart attack.

I rushed to Mtwara, with the little money that I had saved, taking a flight on East African Airways. I spent the night in Mtwara and the following day I took the first bus for Kitama, the village where my parents had settled. By then my father had been released from Ndanda Mission Hospital, and I saw him at home. He looked frail and had lost weight since I last saw him, and that spirit of confidence I knew so well was definitely missing. Despite the many failures in life and the inability to come out of the vicious cycle of poverty, my dad had always had an aura that inspired confidence in his children. At that time, in 1968, without any medical knowledge, I sensed somehow that my dad had a few months to live. The beginning of the end had started. It was indeed painful.

In a week's time it was obvious that I could not return to Tanga to continue my secondary education—the money was not there to pay for my upkeep in Tanga. And so my dad and elder brother Aziz planned that I start a small shop in a nearby village some five miles away, to complement our family income. This came as a shock to me. I had left Tanga in a hurry and had not even formalized my exit from the school. I was asked to decide on a life-changing event. I am wary of assigning defining moments in my life since, as you will see, there were many such moments.

Too many influences swirl around us, and other secret ones percolate up from the unconscious. During those sleepless, anxious nights that followed, I started thinking analytically. I started to focus and prioritize my options. This is incredibly difficult. But it is perhaps the most worthy struggle one can undertake in one's life.

I began by reorienting my expectations for my life and choosing what was important. This thought process was something I call "practical enlightenment." Some pain is inevitable—life consists of failures, losses, regrets, and deaths. I confronted my dad and Aziz and told them I did not want to get into the dukawalla (small shop) business, I wanted to continue with my education no matter what. Reluctantly my opinion was respected. The next day in a rented pickup I left with my brother for Masasi, a small town in the interior of the southern region of the country. From Masasi we went on to Chidya Secondary School, which was some twenty miles away, though it took us almost four hours to reach it, the road was so bad.

Chidya Secondary School (CSS) was known before independence (1961) as Saint Joseph's College. I was extremely lucky that afternoon, because the headmaster was able to call the Ministry of Education in Dar es Salaam and get permission to accept me as a Form III student. Thus I did my Forms III and IV at CSS.

3

Chidya Secondary School

One day in retrospect the years of struggle will strike you
as the most beautiful.

SIGMUND FREUD

The time spent at Chidya Secondary School was extremely important in my growth and progress. I had some memorable moments
there in spite of its distance from urban life. The most difficult and
stressful moments of our life can end up being the most formative
and motivating.

Chidya Secondary School, some twenty miles from Masasi, was
owned and managed by the Anglican Church. It was a boarding
school and therefore a prison without bars in the middle of nowhere,
surrounded by a dense tropical jungle. The nearest settlement in the
1960s was some five miles away, a small village named Chiwata. The
location of the school had been chosen based on the availability of
water, two miles downhill, where there was a natural water reservoir
formed by the streams from where we got our water supply. This
natural reservoir was called Kambona.

In 1969 the school had eight classes, two for each form, and
there were 280 students. I was the first and only student of Indian

heritage, an "Asian," the rest were Africans from different parts of Tanzania, including the far north around Lake Victoria. The conditions here were harsh. There was a deep-rooted tradition of bullying, with Form I (grade nine) bearing the brunt. Form IV had a lot of privileges. Food seemed unfit for human consumption—the only way I could eat it was by adding really hot chilies (pilipili mbuzi) to it, and the habit of eating hot chilies with my food has persisted until today. We were given mainly kidney beans (more often than not, rotten) with ugali, a traditional maize meal staple.

On the first day of my arrival I had to sleep on a metal spring with only a thin bedsheet on it, and because of the altitude of the place, Chidya was very cold at night. On arrival I shed tears, and two years later when I left, paradoxically I cried again. On that first day, my neighbour in the dorm saw my plight of having no mattress and early the next morning the two of us went to the nearby forest to cut grass. The grass was spread to dry, and in the evening he brought two large gunny sacks which we filled with the dry grass. The open ends of the sacks were then stitched together to form one big mattress. I used this mattress for two years and had the best sleep ever. Once a month on a Sunday I had to bring this mattress out and keep it under the hot sun, so that insects would not become my permanent sleeping partners.

My assertion is that anyone who has survived CSS in the sixties should be able to survive anywhere in the world. Today when I sit with my grandkids and tell them about my time in CSS, they are amazed. I wonder if they believe me.

Before ending my time in Chidya, while I was in Form IV, preparing for the final Cambridge School Certificate examination, I suffered from a severe attack of malaria. I was hospitalized in the school clinic for two days and was treated, I think, with intravenous quinine. This was the fourth malaria attack that I can recall: the first one was in Matombo in 1962, the second in Tanga in 1964, the third in Mtwara in 1966. This one in Chidya was the most severe. These four encounters with malaria may be the reason why I chose fighting this disease as my future career, not that I recall any such thoughts while I was suffering.

Two things I need to point out about CSS. The first is that the quality of education was excellent. Despite the severe living conditions, the education was the best. There was no reason for failure—every day except Sundays we had private study time between seven and nine PM, which was spent on homework and extra learning. There was no shortage of textbooks, the laboratories were well equipped, and we had the best teachers, including Peace Corps volunteers, other expatriates, and qualified local teachers.

The second thing was that at CSS I learned determination. Firmness of purpose and resoluteness should not only be a thought process. For the first time I felt I could touch determination and it was a strong, pulsating feeling. For the rest of my life, my currency has been determination: whenever I am determined to achieve something I succeed. I appreciated meritocracy and realized that there is no penalty for overachievement. I remember my mom telling me to always strive to score more goals in soccer in case the referee disallowed a few.

Apart from determination, I realized that consistency is what transforms average into excellence. I also learned to be disciplined, focused, time-conscious, and organized. At CSS, I learned to set goals and worked until I had accomplished them. Because of the conditions, how to survive was a constant battle and this indeed erased one's ego. I think ego is perhaps at the core of all human misunderstandings, and fortunately I had the opportunity to address ego while still a teenager. While this description might make the ego seem like a static thing, it is not. Rather, it is an active and dynamic part of our personalities, playing an immense role in creating emotional drama in our lives. For those who have a strong faith in their religion, ego means Edging God Out.

Tanzania in the late sixties was adopting socialist ideology and there was a fair amount of brainwashing and propaganda. In early 1970 a guest came to visit us from the ruling party, The Tanganyika African National Union (TANU). Tanzania was a single-party nation. Our guest was with us for two weeks and his objective was to instill in us the current political ideology. For two weeks, from morning till evening, we were given political propaganda. We were woken up at 4:30 AM and taken on a five-mile run in the jungle in darkness. The risk of snake bites was high. This run in Kiswahili was known as mchaka-mchaka, and while we ran we had to loudly sing political songs. One of the popular songs was

Kwenye kikundi cha siasa Nyerere yupo! (In the group of politicians Nyerere is present!).

After the run, classes started, and they were sheer political brainwashing. Later we were taught parade drills and practiced for hours. Finally after two weeks we performed the march past parade in the Chinese military style. We were also taught to create Swahili political poetry (mashairi), and I composed one which I sang during the final parade. It was in a question-answer mode.

Mpendwa mwanasiasa,
ondoa yangu mashaka,
eleza kinaganaga,
kichwani mnaniwasha,
jinsi gani watu wote ni sawa.

dear politician,
remove my suspicions,
my head is itching,

clearly explain
how people are equal

This political education was very useful later on in my life when I became interested in politics.

In 1969 there was a severe drought. The water level in our reservoir was low and the pump at the reservoir, which was two miles downhill, could not bring us water from its low level. Each student had to go down to the reservoir to fetch a bucket of water for cooking purposes. This was a tough task but it had to be done, otherwise there was no food. One day I carried a full bucket and before submitting it I wanted to use a little water for my personal use. While I went to fetch a container another student took my bucket and went to the bathing shed for a bath. I followed him and after exchanging blows I was able to rescue my water bucket. Unintentionally one of my blows struck his forehead and this resulted in a bleeding cut of about seven inches. He was taken to the clinic to get his wound stitched. From that day I established my superiority in physical strength and daring. No one could bully me or take me for a ride. It seemed that in African traditions blood is an ominous sign.

My Cambridge School Certificate examinations were in October that year. I had done well in the mock examination and was well prepared for the final. These were my last and sad days at CSS. I was so used to life here that I did not miss urban life.

In those days, based upon the results of the mock examination, almost 80% of the students were selected either for further schooling (Form V), to go to a college, or for a direct administrative position in a government office. I was selected to go to Dar es Salaam Technical College to pursue a three-year diploma course in laboratory technology. It would enable me to manage a scientific laboratory in secondary schools.

Once again I had to leave my comfort zone, but first I went to Mtwara, where my family had moved and had a small shop. Our family had grown, because my sister Gulshan, her husband, and her three children had joined us. We were nine in the small house. My brother was employed in a state business enterprise as a salesman. During this brief break, before I left for Dar es Salaam, I helped in the shop, which was very similar to the one we had owned in Morogoro.

One afternoon, on Monday December 22, my dad called me to sit with him, and he started a philosophical discussion. He began by telling me that a small child trying to learn to walk will fall down and hurt himself maybe hundreds of times, but at no point does that child ever stop and think, Oh I guess walking is not for me, I am not good at it. His message was clear—keep on the struggle till you achieve.

Next we discussed moderation. It did not apply to smoking or drinking alcohol. Had I paid heed to his advice about smoking and drinking, perhaps I would have been in better physical shape now and perhaps avoided my type-two diabetes.

That very afternoon, at around four PM, he was hospitalized due to chest pain. As he was getting into the car to go to the hospital, he turned his head and gave me a smile. It was the last I saw him alive.

Next morning I went to the hospital and was informed that he had passed away during the night. The knowledge that he was no longer there to advise me was overwhelming, and I was in tears. But the province of death is portable, it seems. I became haunted by an overpowering sense of gloom: My father does not exist anymore. There is nothing left. He is leading to where one day I will follow. But how can I follow, when there is no tomorrow? How will there be tomorrow without my dear father? Ours was a big family, and our social life like that of most families of modest means who grew up in the small towns and villages, revolved around meals, conversations, and storytelling. I had never had any holiday outing with my parents, we did not have television—the first television I bought was in 1985. Despite this, I feel that we grew up in a happy environment. I learned a lot from the stories and mealtime conversations. I understood that no one is perfect but most people are good, people should not be judged by their worst or weakest moments, and being harsh in our judgments can turn us into hypocrites, and a lot of life is just showing up and hanging on, and laughter is often the best medicine for pain. Most importantly, everyone has a tale to tell about dreams and nightmares, hope and heartache, love and loss, courage and fear, sacrifice and selfishness. These discussions may have played a big role in shaping my personality and perhaps even my future endeavours. Some stories were myths but very fascinating. When I recall my life today I am reminded of Augustus Caesar who is supposed to have said: "I found Rome a city of bricks and left it a city of marble." No screen time or Nintendo game can teach a teenager such wisdom.

My father through discussions taught me to be practical rather than emotional, to be positive but not to force myself to stay positive all the time because that would be to deny the existence of life's problems. When you deny your problems you rob yourself of the chance to solve them and generate happiness. Problems add a sense of meaning and importance to our life. To duck our problems is to lead a meaningless, even if supposedly pleasant, existence.

There is no correct dogma or perfect ideology. There is only what your experience has shown you to be right for you. Since we all have differing needs and personal experiences we will all inevitably come to differing correct answers. Certainty is the enemy of growth. Nothing is for certain until it has already happened and even then it's still debatable. That's why accepting the inevitable imperfections of our values is necessary for any growth to take place.

Instead of striving for certainty we should be in constant search for doubt: doubt about our own beliefs, doubt about our own feelings, doubt about what the future may hold for us unless we get out there and create it for ourselves. Instead of looking to be right all the time we should be looking for where we are wrong because we often are. No matter how honest and well intentioned we are, we are in a perpetual state of misleading ourselves and others for no other reason than that our brain is designed to be efficient but not precise.

All this I learned from a man who never had formal education. In silence, many a time I try to eulogize my dad. I would like to remember him simply as a good and decent man, but I would not like to idealize or enlarge him in death beyond what he was in life.

As I previously said, in real life my dad was tall, strong, and hefty. He was a very simple and honest man, always smiling despite the harsh realities and challenges he was facing. Though he had this pleasant personality he was very strict with us, his children. His understanding of poverty was somehow weird. He said that poverty consists not in the decrease of one's possessions, but in the increase of one's greed. As I reflect today, I think he was a zealous adherent of our faith, there was no compromise in his religious belief. From him I learned and cultivated such habits as nonviolence, truthfulness, honesty, cleanliness, contentment, self-discipline and a compelling desire to reach my goals. With so much wisdom and integrity that he possessed, I cannot explain why he never succeeded in life and why failure was like his shadow. Maybe he was just unlucky.

Fifty years on, with a forty-year-old son and two grandchildren I still miss my father.

Within two weeks I had to leave for Dar es Salaam to pursue my technical studies. My brother bought me an airline ticket and gave me forty-five shillings (about six American dollars), to carve out my own life.

4

Dar es Salaam in the Seventies

Asiyejua utu si mtu.
(One who does not know humaneness is not human.)

SWAHILI PROVERB

Straight from the airport the taxi took me to Dar es Salaam Technical College at the corner of Morogoro Road and Bibi Titi Mohamed Road. Dar es Salaam, more sophisticated and much larger than any place I had lived in before, brought me many new and exciting experiences. I would lead a completely independent life and make my own decisions about my future. I would make new friends. In 1970 the population of Dar was less than half a million, which seemed large; today it is approaching seven million people.

I did not have shoes when I left Mtwara, wearing open sandals, so I had to buy leather shoes for thirty shillings from a shop located in Jiwan Hirji Building; the shop is still there. I was left with about ten shillings in my pocket for my expenses, though meals and accommodation were provided at no cost. Meals were much better than at Chidya Secondary. At the end of the month each student received forty-five shillings as monthly allowance from the government. I was happy, and soon I started playing ping pong and basketball.

But my stay at Technical College was short, because I was not happy with the course I was pursuing, training to become a laboratory technician for secondary schools. I was more ambitious. By chance, one day I met a classmate from Chidya, and he encouraged me to apply to Muhimbili Hospital. I applied and was selected to appear for an interview for a course in medical laboratory technology. This was a three-year course. The interview was straightforward and I was selected to join immediately.

The problem was, how to leave DTC, since I had government sponsorship? I was required to inform the Ministry of Education and request permission to change my training. Doing so would delay my exit, and permission could be denied. I decided to leave without informing anyone, and in those days it was difficult to track anyone. The next day I threw my bag over the fence onto a public pathway and went through the gate round the college, picked up my bag and went straight to the hostel of the Muhimbili Faculty of Medicine to start my new life. This was in February 1970, and I would leave Muhimbili in June 2013. Some forty-three years and four months of my life were spent there. I consider this period as my second phase in life.

Muhimbili is one of the oldest medical institutions in the country. Formerly it was known as Princess Margaret Hospital, because it was opened by Princess Margaret when she visited the country in colonial times; the name was changed at the time of independence. Today it is known as the Muhimbili National Hospital. The Muhimbili campus consists of the teaching hospital and the medical university, i.e. Muhimbili University of Health and Allied Sciences (MUHAS), but when I joined it, it was administratively the Faculty of Medicine under the University of Dar es Salaam (UDSM). Until 1977 UDSM was part of the East African Universities.

It was UDSM that had sponsored me for a certificate course;

upon completion I was required to work for five years at the teaching laboratories of the Faculty of Medicine. Sponsored students were accommodated at the medical students hostel while those sponsored by the Ministry of Health were accommodated in the allied science hostel. Our training took place at the Central Pathology Laboratory (CPL). This was a newly built laboratory funded by the German Government.

As students we had to rotate on a monthly basis in each pathology department. There was a media and sterilization department, where we prepared media for bacterial growth and provided the hospital with sterile universal bottles for collecting body fluids. There was a lot of work on a daily basis, but the most important part of it was quality assurance of the entire process of sterilization. The department lab had a characteristic smell, which even today lingers in me, evoking memories of that period in my life.

The other departments were involved with biochemistry, histology, microbiology, blood transfusion, hematology, serology, and parasitology. This last subject fascinated me the most, because parasites in different stages of their development in blood, urine, and stool samples can be observed under a microscope. But it needs much practice and skill, and also the understanding of the diagnosis of parasitic infection.

We were allowed to find our own accommodation off campus if we wished, and received a stipend of 350 shillings a month. I opted to stay as a paying guest with a very good family on Uhuru Street in Kariakoo. It was a middle-class Asian family with husband, wife, and three small children. The husband was self-employed, buying and selling whatever was available in the market, and it seemed he was not making much profit so his wife supplemented by keeping paying guests. There were five of us staying as paying guests paying 250 shillings per month. We were like her family, she was very kind and treated us well.

The main reason I opted to leave the hostel at Muhimbili was because my mother had moved to Dar es Salaam and I had to pay for her expenses. After my dad passed away in December 1970, our small shop closed and my sister's family decided to relocate to Dar es Salaam. My brother Aziz and my mom moved to a rented house. At that time my other elder brother Shamshun was working as an agriculture extension officer in Lindi town while Nizar was a motor mechanic in Arusha.

My mom was suffering from frequent acute abdominal pains. (Much later at Muhimbili she was diagnosed with gallbladder inflammation and stones and had surgery to remove the gallbladder.) And so while I was still studying at Muhimbili I had to take care of her. She was staying with her niece as a paying guest, and I had to pay her rent of 200 shillings. To add to my meager allowance, I worked in the evenings as a doorkeeper at Chox Cinema for a salary of 75 shillings per month, with the privilege of seeing movies at no cost in all the theatres in the city. I worked at Chox with my close friend Nazmu.

Nazmu hailed from Mtwara. While I was in Chidya, he was in a private secondary school in the nearby town of Lindi. In 1970, conforming to the socialist ideology of the country, there occurred en-masse nationalizations of private houses and this had a very negative impact on the Asian population. It resulted in many families migrating from the interior of Tanzania to the capital, Dar es Salaam, and gradually on to some countries in the West.

Nazmu was very disciplined, a fitness freak, and like me he was also working to get some extra money to support his family. Unlike me, after completing his Cambridge School Certificate he went for direct employment as a supervisor in a shirt factory.

Nowadays I meet Nazmu in Calgary once in a while at

Headquarters Jamatkhana and we often reminisce about our happier past. Like me he has two grandchildren and stays with his family somewhere in Chestermere, just outside Calgary.

In 1974, while on a night call in the department of blood transfusion at Muhimbili, a man from the Aga Khan Welfare Society approached me with an urgent request for blood of a rare group for a pregnant woman at the Aga Khan Hospital. That night the blood bank at Muhimbili had more than enough blood units, so I gave them two units of the required blood. This favour led to a very fulfilling ten-year involvement with the Aga Khan Welfare Society. I was appointed as a health convener and my responsibility was to look after a number of community members regarding their mental and physical health. This was a voluntary position and for the first time I became involved in providing professional services. In this engagement I learned a lot about service and how to deal with people in a humble manner. I also made lifelong friends with whom I interact even today. One particular person was the gentleman who had initially approached me for the blood. His name is Shiraz Mitha and he currently lives in Sydney, Australia.

Life has to move forward and when I was in my third year at Muhimbili I got a part-time job as a medical laboratory technician in a private hospital known as the K K Khan Hospital. The salary was 350 shillings per month. I quit the job at Chox cinema, my earnings quadrupled, the job was prestigious, and I was now learning how to manage a clinical laboratory.

Some time in 1973, while working at K K Khan, I met a woman, Zeenat, who became my girlfriend and later my life partner. Zeenat was working at the National Bank of Commerce branch as a cashier; later she became branch manager for foreign currency. I knew her as a neighbour who lived in an adjacent building on Uhuru Street. I used to see her often walking by my building, but I had made no attempt to speak to her even though I found her pretty and liked her. One day I learned from a colleague at K K Khan that Zeenat's mother was sick. I gathered the courage to approach her and inquire about her mother. It turned out that she was suffering from epilepsy and needed to be seen by a neurologist. I arranged this and accompanied Zeenat and her mother to see the neurologist at Muhimbili Hospital. This small favour resulted in our lifelong partnership which is still flourishing after forty-four years.

Zeenat was beautiful (I know that beauty is in the beholder's eye but I was the beholder). In the beginning she was in my heart, but before I knew it, she became my soul mate. She was a truly remarkable person, soft spoken, quiet and observant but smart, tough, and a brilliant worker. In short a very spiritual being and a kindred soul. Her family consisted only of herself and her mother; her father had passed away when she was eight years old. We got married on July 31, 1976.

I successfully completed my certificate training in 1974 and was posted as lab technician in the Department of Parasitology and Medical Entomology within the Faculty of Medicine at Muhimbili Hospital.

In the final examination of the course we were given two samples of urine on which to perform pregnancy tests. My results were both negative, but almost all the other students became wary of getting the same result and therefore wrote one positive result for one of the samples. When we walked out of the exam, I was in real distress because of this. But later I came to know that both samples had been from the same male. This was an important lesson, that science does not follow the majority, like in politics; one needs evidence to make an inference.

My life now changed drastically because I had secure employment and my monthly salary was 980 shillings (about $130). I started looking for a house and was able to get a two-room apartment on the third floor of a building on Nkrumah Street. I stayed there for over forty years.

Sometime in 1975, I was transferred from Parasitology and Medical Entomology to start a new clinical laboratory in the department of pediatrics. Meanwhile I had also started a diploma course of two years in parasitology with the gut feeling that this would be my future career. Choosing a career is like choosing a wife from ten girlfriends. Even if you pick the most beautiful and intelligent and the kindest woman, there is still the pain of losing the other nine.

This was my second qualification, an East African University diploma in medical laboratory technology specializing in parasitology. I have always mentioned these two qualifications, a certificate and a diploma, in my resume and some of my colleagues have told me to drop them, since I had already moved on and achieved higher degrees. My reply has been, *Usiache mbachao kwa msala upitao,* meaning, Don't throw away your rag for a borrowed mat.

In the department of pediatrics I taught laboratory tests to postgraduate students and analyzed clinical samples for the department. I will forever remember the Head of the Department, the Late Professor Kimati, internationally renowned pediatrician, who was extremely honest, humble and wise.

Professor Kimati did research on malnutrition and parasitic infections and had collected about 3000 blood slides to detect malaria parasites. This was in 1977. One day he brought the slides to me and said, "I know this is a lot of work, take your time—but I have no money to pay you for this extra work. In case I get the research grant I will definitely pay you; or else you could wait until I get the grant and then you can start the work." I had the option of storing the slides until that day, but I went ahead and examined about fifty slides a day. In three months when I gave him the results, he was extremely surprised that I had done the work; a few days later he informed me that he had randomly chosen a hundred of the slides and had them reread as quality control, and the results were very good.

In 1980 he called me to his office and asked me if I wanted to join the university and pursue medical studies. He would gladly recommend me. In just two days I was accepted as a student to pursue an undergraduate degree in medicine, for the degree of Doctor of Medicine. This was a five-year course and would be followed by one year of internship. The government would provide free accommodation (medical students had to stay on the campus) and meals and an allowance of 350 shillings. And so I started my medical studies.

Zeenat quit her job at the bank and took up a better-paid position at the French oil company TOTAL Tanzania, where she went on to work for forty years. For the next five years she was the main bread earner of our family. In January 1978, two years after our wedding, we welcomed a healthy son, who has continued even now to bring boundless and cosmic happiness in our family. We named him Zainil. Our family got somehow stuck on the letter Z. I, my wife, my son, and now both our grandchildren have names that start with Z. I was now supporting a typical extended family, consisting of my mother, my mother-in-law, my niece and my nephew, all staying with us in our apartment. On the first day of my medical studies I had to drop Zainil at his pre-school. Pursuing education has no age limits.

I had a room in the hostel and for the first three years of my medical course I literally lived in the hostel, going home in the early mornings to drop my son to nursery school. In my second year, in 1982, one day Professor Kimati came looking for me in the hostel. I was surprised and a bit fearful, but he had come to inform me that he was leaving the country to go to Bangladesh as a WHO Director of a Diarrheal Centre. He gave me a brand new Kawasaki motorbike as a gift, because I had read the blood slides without asking for money. A year later I sold the motorbike for 300,000 shillings. This was a lot of money.

5

Life As a Medical Student

Elimu ndio mwanga uongozayo kila shani.
(Knowledge is the light that leads everywhere.)

SWAHILI PROVERB

Joining the medical faculty was a big step in my life. It brought many changes and sacrifices, not only from me but all my family members. Many nights, in silence, when everyone else was asleep in our house, I would think about my decision. I had an advantage, because I knew the Muhimbili campus well and most of the lecturers, as well as the system of teaching. The attrition rate was about fifty percent in the first two years, hence time commitment and hard work were at the core of any success. Some lecturers, especially in the clinical departments, treated students with scorn, in the apparent belief that insulting other people's intelligence was a way to assert their own authority. Notwithstanding all these issues, this was an opportunity that I would not be able to get anywhere else in the world. I know of no other place in the world that gives you money to study medicine; this could happen only in Tanzania, and I am deeply grateful.

I had become aware that medicine is a science of uncertainty, and an art of probability (Sir William Osler). One big plus that I had observed during my stay at Muhimbili was that modern medical training required that compassion was important (except for the arrogance of some lecturers). I saw senior medical students show empathy for their patients, being sensitive and caring. To me these values were very important.

At that time the medical curriculum was different from what it is at present. We had assessment tests every Saturday morning from eight to eleven AM. Usually two subjects were tested, on material covered in the past two or three weeks. These test marks contributed sixty percent to the final mark of a student. Initially there was a lot of rote learning, but slowly some subjects like physiology became more concept based. Some rote learning, of course, is essential: for example, the anatomy of the human being has to become second nature, and the life cycles of organisms have to be at one's fingertips. I struggled with biochemistry initially, because I lacked a strong background in inorganic chemistry. But I worked very hard and passed all the subjects.

This was a big relief and the ensuing two months of vacation after the first year were well deserved. I was able to give the family quality time. It was a joy to play with my son, who was now approaching his fourth birthday.

There were field trips in the following years, and I appreciated them. The second-year field trip involved community nutrition assessment in children under five years. Our class in 1982 went to what is now Mkuranga District. We were divided into groups of seven, with a faculty member as our supervisor. Each group was based in a village along the Mkuranga-Kisiju road. Kisiju is on the coast of the Indian Ocean. The groups were accommodated in the primary schools in each village, when they were on vacation. I was stationed at Mkuranga Primary School. We collected data like the weights, heights, mid-arm circumferences of randomly selected children under five years of age. Other social and demographic data was also collected. This was analyzed on a daily basis and after six days of data collection we met with the community to give them feedback. This introductory field trip was holistic because we learned how to answer a research question, collect systematic data, analyze the data, and communicate feedback. We were also introduced to community social life and to observe how illness starts within a community. It was a very enjoyable and instructive stay in Mkuranga.

The third-year field trip had a different goal. We had to assess the prevalence of a communicable disease in the community. Our class in 1983 went to Dodoma region (Dodoma is now the political capital). Again we were divided into groups of seven. Each group was in a village along the Dodoma-Manyoni road. The first group was at Bahi, followed by Kintinku, Maweni and Kilimatinde villages. I was at Maweni. This field trip was more comprehensive because we collected stool and urine specimens to detect urinary and intestinal schistosomiasis. In each village we had a mobile laboratory to process the specimens and those found positive were treated. We also collected data about water supply, use of toilets, and variables pertaining to household income. Again this field trip was a very good learning exercise and we had a wonderful time in the field. Dodoma region is well known for its meat industry and we had a goat feast and generous drinking every night. The bus trip from Dar es Salaam to Dodoma in those days took a good twelve to fourteen hours.

Much later, in 2000, when I was a faculty member, I was selected to lead a similar field trip for the third-year medical students. Because the class size was more than 200 students, we went to Mtwara town. I was in a very good position to assess the benefits of this field trip compared to the one I had gone on as a medical student, and my recommendation was rather negative based on a cost-benefit ratio. These field trips are very costly. Their primary objective, to observe the dynamics of disease-community interaction, including social determinants, was not achieved this time because of the number of students.

In the fourth year there was a two-month rotation in community health, during which we had to spend one week at a district hospital and write a report that was graded.

I was with a fellow student, Lahar Ngubeni who was from South Africa. Tanzania was a main hub for South African freedom fighters and we hosted them very cordially. Many of them joined our institutions of higher learning. The two of us travelled to Muheza District in Tanga region, where I had spent a part of my childhood. We were hosted by the DMO—the District Medical Officer—and for a week we had a room in the nursing college. Muheza District Hospital was a "designated" hospital, meaning that it was initially run by a Christian mission but now the public sector was in partnership. In Tanzania in the eighties several districts had no district hospital but they had mission managed hospitals. In such places the government created a partnership with the mission and such hospitals were referred to as designated hospitals. Part of the hospital budget was covered by the government.

We arrived in the evening and at around eight PM, while we were seated outside in the veranda playing chess, the nurse came and said there was an emergency in the obstetric ward. There was no one else available, and since we were doctors from the prestigious Muhimbili Hospital we could help. We had just passed through our fourth-year obstetrics and gynecology rotation, so we agreed. It turned out to be a case of obstructed labour and an urgent Cesarean section was needed to save the mother and her child. We decided to take it on.

In that rotation we had observed many cesarean sections and also had performed a few under supervision. So here we were, supposedly doctors, to perform for the first time an unsupervised caesarian section. To top our predicament, there was no one to give anesthesia. So my colleague, Ngubeni, gave anesthesia and I performed the Caesarian section.

All went well, the child was delivered with an Apgar score of 7 (i.e. it was a healthy baby). The problem started when it was finally time to stitch the skin. The needle was blunt and therefore the patient would feel a lot of pain. There was no way I could go ahead using the blunt needle. The assisting nurse then gave me a new hypodermic needle and taught me to stitch one suture at a time, which I did. The mother and newborn did well and were discharged on the fourth day without any postoperative infection.

In medical training, where skill training is required, the best teacher is not the professor but a hands-on nurse. It is the nurses who save many lives by finding the vein for intravenous infusion at the most critical time. Treating a patient is teamwork, but the qualified doctor not only takes the credit but also the bigger chunk of payment. Whoever said the world was a fair playground?

I was so overwhelmed with learning and the new information that came all the time at lightning speed that I did not notice the passage of time. Soon I was a fifth-year student and the final qualifying examination was at hand. There was a lot of fear and anxiety about the examinations. I managed to clear all the subjects except pediatrics, where during the clinical examination I made a fatal error that cost me eight weeks of extra time. All my life I have treated more pediatric patients than adults because malaria is basically a childhood illness in endemic areas. And so the extra eight weeks that I spent in pediatrics turned out to be useful in my later working life.

While most of my classmates started their internships in August 1985, I started my internship in late September. We all graduated in the first week of December with MD degrees from the University of Dar es Salaam. The Chancellor was President Julius Nyerere, popularly known as Mwalimu and the Father of the Nation. If I recall correctly, ours was the last graduation ceremony he attended, because after that he voluntarily stepped down as president of the United Republic of Tanzania.

A year of internship: a stress-free time

I started my internship in pediatrics to ensure continuity in my learning of diseases affecting childhood health. The internship, which was at Muhimbili, was very demanding physically. We had to rotate in all clinical departments, some had one-month rotations, some had two, and in the bigger departments like Obstetrics & Gynecology, the rotation lasted three months.

Because there were a small number of interns, at times there would be only one intern per department, which meant that he or she was on call seven days a week. One consulting firm (firm C) within the department of Obstetrics & Gynecology had a ninety-six-hour period of admission on a weekend, meaning that for one weekend every month the firm would be responsible for new admissions from Friday morning through to Monday morning, thus the intern slogged like a donkey. I believe these days the International Labor Organization would not allow this working condition. However, there were no examinations. The learning curve was really steep, every day I learned new things and the skills I learned for practical work tremendously improved my abilities. There was a lot of satisfaction from the clinical work, because there were serious patients who were hospitalized, and when they got well and were discharged, they would express profound gratitude. Nothing can compare to that feeling for a doctor.

I will relay one unique incident. During my surgical rotation, we had to see new patients at the casualty and decide whether to admit them or not. At about midnight one day a young couple with their parents and their six-month-old child came. The child was crying loudly, and this had been going on, they said, for the past three hours. The mother said that the child was also pulling his left ear, so perhaps there was something wrong there. This was not a surgical patient, but since I was in the casualty department awaiting patients, the nurse politely requested me if I could assist. As taught in the clinical rotations, always start to examine the normal side first. So I examined the right ear with the otoscope and saw a live cockroach in the external ear. With a forceps I pulled the cockroach out and luckily it came out live and unbroken. The family started shouting and running amok. It took some time for the nurses and other staff to calm them so I could speak to them. The issue was that they thought I was some sort of a magician, to pull a cockroach that had entered the left ear from the right ear. It all ended up as a funny midnight episode. I was able to allay their concerns with the correct explanation. This was something not uncommon. Once the cockroach was pulled out, the child immediately stopped crying and later was laughing. All ended well.

One year of internship passed like the blink of an eye. I was ready to start work as a medical officer anywhere in Tanzania, but my interest lay in malaria, in parasitic infections, in teaching and in research. In retirement now, I give below some reflections about medical education in a developing country.

Reflections on medical education in developing countries

As I finished medical school, I started thinking about how medical school could be made more interesting and less of a torture. In the first two years many students seriously contemplate quitting, because there is a lot of memorization and rote-learning for tests

40

rather than critical thinking. Almost all students come into medical school excited about helping people and the intellectual challenge of practicing medicine, but a month into medical school they are disillusioned.

There is a very distinct line drawn across the curriculum, between the preclinical and the clinical. This difference makes the preclinical curriculum rather boring and initially uninspiring. But with time, as knowledge progresses, the teaching becomes more interesting and intellectually stimulating. Eventually one learns to develop differential diagnoses for a constellation of symptoms and determines which is most likely for a given patient. One will be asked to interpret the scientific evidence and determine which treatment is merited for the patient. Maybe one will ask one's own questions and figure out how to answer them.

You'll certainly be asked to help patients and families walk through painful conditions such as cancer, trauma, dementia, and more. But this can feel remote when your main task is to memorize in which chromosome the gene affected in neurofibromatosis type II is located. While I was surprised by how much memorization engulfed my study hours, it was reassuring to know that it had little bearing on my future enjoyment of the practice of medicine.

Perhaps the difference between the preclinical and clinical curricula should be more flexible, and preclinical knowledge should be applied much earlier for patient care. I think a problem-based preclinical curriculum would have made the first two years more interesting and more fruitful. Another thing that I experienced in my first two years was an atmosphere of ruthless competition. The classes were notorious for hypercompetition and perfectionism. This attitude changed during the clinical years and the environment was markedly less competitive, more collaborative, and friendly. Miraculously, the same classmates became my best resource, but I learned more from registrars and residents and I learned the more practical skills from nurses. Medical schools should encourage collaboration, and once a year during the graduation ceremony these less visible team players should be recognized for their contributions. Most students decide their future specialization from experiences and observations made during their undergraduate years. There is very little guidance from the senior teachers to help a student in choosing a future career. I believe there is a need for more initiative to attract graduates into different specialties.

During the orientation week for freshmen, the late Professor Karashani explained to prospective students that in medical school a day needs to have twenty-five hours instead of twenty-four. His intention was good and he meant that in medical training the studies were to be taken very seriously, since the curriculum was tough and very demanding. Perhaps this was not good advice and quite counterproductive. I was a good sportsman in secondary school, but for the five years in medical school I never played any game or went to the sports field.

6

Academic Don

In the faculty of failure, mediocrity is never an optional course.

ISRAELMORE AYIVOR

After internship I was selected to join the Department of Parasitology & Medical Entomology in the medical school as a tutorial assistant. This was in late 1986. My primary job was to assist in teaching undergraduate and postgraduate students. I took this opportunity to read deeply around the subject and became quite proficient. Now that I had my basic MD degree there was no looking back. A world of opportunities was available, but I was interested in working as an academician. And so I enjoyed the teaching. At that time the salary of a tutorial assistant was about 200,000 shillings. I also took a part time clinical job at the Aga Khan Hospital doing night shifts for a total of thirty-six hours a week. This was the first time that I was able to save some money for my family's future.

In September 1988 I received a Tropical Disease Research (TDR/ WHO) scholarship to pursue a master's degree at the prestigious London School of Hygiene & Tropical Medicine. The LSHTM was often called the Mecca for the study of tropical diseases and it was part of the University of London. This was my first trip abroad and it was with much trepidation that I took that flight. It was a wrench to be separated from my young son, but my wife stood by me and encouraged me to go. Going abroad in the late eighties was still a big deal.

I was also fearful about leaving my mom and my mother-in-law. Both were approaching their eighties and needed constant medical care. The option of leaving our elderly parents and going for a greener pasture elsewhere did not exist for me, there was no compromise on this issue with me; besides, I was convinced that it was morally wrong to leave a nation that had invested in me. I had to pay back.

My other reason was that, with my background, nowhere in the world would I have had an opportunity to do medicine. I had this inner calling that I needed to remain in Tanzania and serve the people. This I have done with full commitment. It was not just a matter of remaining in Tanzania. I could easily have started a private practice or joined a private hospital, but I resisted that too. Even today I believe that if education is acquired through taxes paid by the people, one is duty bound to serve them. In all my years I did not experience racism at any pathological level. There was nepotism here and there but nothing that had any impact on my career. At the workplace I was in my comfort zone, outside the workplace there were the occasional racist remarks and profiling, but one soon learns how to interact and neutralize such scenarios.

At LSHTM overall the quality of teaching was very high and the course material was comprehensive. Unfortunately there were a few teachers just like at Muhimbili who were arrogant. They could be ignored. Since I was well prepared I found myself doing well and looked for a part-time job at British Museum which was located nearby.

In those days in Tanzania we still had a monopolized market economy, therefore new or even used cars were not available. It was expected that if you got an opportunity to go abroad, you would come back with a Japanese car. Students who went abroad went to great lengths to save from their meager allowances to be able to purchase a car upon returning. I desired a Japanese car, but I also wanted my wife and son to visit London so that we could have a vacation together. Working part-time enabled me to achieve this. I purchased a Toyota Corolla saloon, which was shipped to Dar es Salaam in late 1989, and Zeenat and Zainil were able to join me in May of that year. We had a wonderful time together. Zeenat's cousin Parviz was staying in East Ham, and she was very helpful, not only during our family vacation but throughout my stay in London. We visited Peterborough, Leicester, and Birmingham and stayed with friends or at cheap motels. It was quality time for us.

Students at LSHTM were allowed to appear for the examination of the advanced Diploma in Tropical Medicine (DTM&H) offered by the Royal College of Physicians. I duly paid the examination fee of 175 pounds and cleared the examination. In September I sat for my final examination for a master's degree, and in November visited friends in Ottawa and Toronto. The primary reason for visiting Canada was to meet old friends, acquaintances, and relatives before returning to Tanzania.

My visit to Canada was a short one. The people were friendly and helpful, but I found Canada to be a very cold country since it was winter. I also noticed that it was expansive and not crowded, the houses were relatively big and comfortable, and the heating system was very efficient. Even when the snow on the rooftops had not melted, the interiors of the houses remained warm. In London, in contrast, heating in the houses was inadequately retained. London was crowded, and there was this feeling of perpetual lack of space.

Houses were small and at times uncomfortable, while outside was mostly wet and hectic. People were abrasive and rude and there was a lot of profiling. There seemed a clear divide of the city along racial lines. Having said this about London, it still seemed that people had learned to coexist, and there was a latent attraction that pulled people towards it. London has its own flavour despite so many negatives.

I was fascinated to see able persons begging at underground train stations—on a small piece of cardboard they would write in large font something like, "Homeless, have not eaten for two day, please contribute, minimum 50 pence." This was something new to me, because back home begging was very different. As I became familiar with this begging pattern, I realized that most of these homeless were using hard narcotics. This was a major public health problem the west was facing, and I saw this begging phenomenon in Boston, New York and other cities. I classified this as the existence of the "fourth world" in the midst of "first world." Years later, when I was the coordinator of a masters degree in public health at Muhimbili, I articulated the public health challenges of the fourth world in the curriculum.

I returned to Dar es Salaam in December 1989 with my MSc degree in Medical Parasitology and a Diploma in Tropical Medicine from Royal College of Physicians.

Back at Muhimbili I was promoted to the rank of lecturer and my teaching assignment increased. I also started supervising postgraduate students. Apart from teaching I was heavily involved in malaria research and became the clinical coordinator and field supervisor in a research project named Bagamoyo BedNet Project (BBNP). Insecticide-treated bed nets were a relatively new concept in malaria control. Ours was among the first few research projects in the world to investigate the impact of this novel intervention on malaria mortality and morbidity.

The Bagamoyo project was funded by USAID, Johns Hopkins School of Public Health (JHSPH) having received the funds to collaborate with Muhimbili University. I will always remain thankful to Professor Clive Shiff of JHSPH and Professor Minjas of the Department of Parasitology & Medical Entomology of Muhimbili University for giving me an opportunity to participate in the project, which covered the whole district of Bagamoyo, which is along the coast north of Dar es Salaam. At that time the road was gravel and it took us about three hours to reach the historical Bagamoyo town sixty kilometres away.

Every week I would spend three or four days in Bagamoyo. I was overseeing the research project, in addition to which for five months a year I conducted mobile malaria clinics in eight villages. In each village we had a cohort of about fifty children under the age of five, and these children were followed up on a weekly basis to assess the impact of insecticide-treated bed nets. We were also assessing the impact of this innovation on the vector population (anopheline mosquitoes). This was indeed a huge research project that lasted for about five years, and resulted in thirty scientific publications. More importantly, the evidence it brought out was fundamental to the fact that today for sub-Saharan African countries it is established policy to use insecticide-treated nets for the control of malaria.

As an individual researcher I benefited immensely from the project. Apart from the publications, which enabled me to become a senior lecturer and later an associate professor, I became internationally recognized as a dedicated malaria researcher and have served in many scientific committees and travelled across the globe.

There are a few issues that I would like to note that directly resulted from the BBNP.

The first of these is how the local population perceives malaria and its treatment options. Once, while in a mobile clinic in Yombo, a village in Bagamoyo District, a child of about six months started having epileptic seizures while waiting in the line to see me. The mother of the child was about fifteen years of age. Immediately after the nurse brought the boy's condition to my attention, I could have easily stopped the seizures by giving intravenous injection of diazepam. This was a typical case of febrile convulsion associated with malaria, which of course had to be treated. I had to inject diazepam intravenously, but this was a point of contention. The local population believed that seizures (dege dege) were caused by witchcraft and injections were fatal. The village leader (in Tanzania every village has a chairman), who over time due to research project activities had become a friend, objected to my intervention but the child's mother wanted me to go ahead with the treatment. In the village set-up the leaders and elders have the last word and are the final decision-makers. The child was taken to a nearby house. I was able to convince the leader that I wanted to go and see what would happen to the child, and he agreed, because he also needed transport. The first decision the elders made was that the mother should urinate on the child. She did that and the seizures stopped immediately. This might be a surprise but it is well known that lowering fever does stop seizure, so actually by urinating on the child the body temperature decreased and the seizures stopped temporarily.

Next I was requested to take the child and the elders in my car to the traditional healer (fundi), who lived two hours away in the jungle. When we arrived at the healer's compound, there were many other patients and there was a lot of activity. As soon as the traditional healer saw the child, he gave him a potion about a quarter cup full to drink. For a more specific treatment, the healer went out into the forest to dig some roots and prepare a liquid potion to chase away the demons. It took him another two hours, thus there was a total delay of about five hours since the onset of the convulsions. Unfortunately for the little boy, delay in starting treatment is the main cause of malaria mortality.

When it started getting dark I asked to leave and they agreed. The group would stay in the healer's compound. In the morning I was told that the child had died. It was a sad moment, especially since I knew that I could have saved the boy. I was also angry, but this is the system in situ, and despite doctors, the majority of the people go to the traditional healers to treat seizures. It would be suicidal for me to preach otherwise. Instead I built a friendly relationship with the traditional healers and asked them to ensure that everyone in their clinic used insecticide-treated nets (ITNs), and secondly to give any child with fever chloroquine tablets (that was the first line drug at that time). Fortunately chloroquine was widely known in the community.

Many years later home-based treatment of malaria by community workers and even traditional healers became a big topic for researchers. I also learned to respect the existing community systems and to proceed very slowly and cautiously to institute any change. I increasingly became interested in the relationship of social science and the practice of modern medicine.

Let me narrate an example. Initially the uptake of ITNs was good, but the re-treatment of nets every six months was not as good. Therefore in the village of Mlingotini I approached the imam (priest) of a mosque and requested him to preach about malaria prevention using ITNs in his Friday khutba (sermon). He agreed and did a very good job. Social scientists in our group evaluated the impact of similar initiatives in a number of mosques and we published the findings. Following publication, I received a number of queries from medical doctors in the United Arab Emirates inquiring about the study. In their region migrant workers from the Indian subcontinent had a habit of chewing tobacco and betel leaves (paan), which can cause oral cancer. They too wanted to use mosques to raise awareness.

Malaria has a number of enigmas, and diagnosis is one of them. In the 1980s, diagnosis was a major hurdle. It consisted of taking a drop of blood from a finger prick and applying a smear on a slide, which was then dried, stained, and viewed under a high-power microscope. This was a lengthy procedure of about an hour and prone to errors, so that false positive results were very common. There was therefore a lot of chloroquine misuse.

As a fourth-year medical student in my pediatric rotation I had done a minor project about chloroquine use. There were some fifty patients. One had had a snake bite and another had symptoms of drowning. Despite this, they were both given chloroquine. That was the extent of chloroquine misuse and the diagnostic conundrum. There was no simple point of care test (PoC) that could differentiate a malaria-positive patient from a negative one.

In 1992 because of my involvement with the Bagamoyo BedNet Project with Johns Hopkins University, I was required to go to Baltimore for a research meeting. A smaller meeting was arranged there with scientists from Becton, Dickinson and Company, a medical technology firm that had successfully developed monoclonal antibodies against the malaria surface antigen on the red blood cell. The question was how to deploy this antibody for diagnostic purposes. A simple system using laminated fibre was developed by scientists from that company. We were the pioneers who tested this new system. The first paper on this topic was published by us and provided evidence that this was a successful diagnostic tool for malaria.

Since this publication, thousands of papers have followed on the subject, and now the test is popularly known as a Rapid Diagnostic Test (RDT) and is deployed globally for malaria diagnosis. Millions of these RDTs are used every year in sub-Saharan Africa. I feel proud that I was involved in this research, but my entrepreneurial skills are poor and I failed to capitalize on the monetary aspect of this opportunity.

A third issue that emanated from BBNP further shaped my life as a malaria researcher. In 1994 I published a paper on anaemia from data obtained from my BBNP work.

This paper caught the attention of Professor Anders Björkman of Karolinska Institutet (KI) in Stockholm. This resulted in a very constructive collaboration that lasted until I retired. There was a new regulation at Muhimbili that for promotion one had to have a PhD. Just at that time, in 1994, Professor Björkman offered to take me as a PhD student in Sweden.

There are a number of systems for PhD studies, but in Sweden the PhD is obtained mainly through the publication of research papers. My research was to be conducted in Tanzania, while the data analysis and writing for publication had to be done at KI in Stockholm. Additionally, it was a requirement for candidates to obtain a certain number of points from attending recommended courses, including scientific philosophy, advanced epidemiology, and statistics.

In 1995, then, I visited KI and was teamed with a Swedish PhD student, Ekvall Hakan, who was a medical doctor. We wrote up a proposal for work to be funded by the Swedish aid agency SIDA/SAREC and we started work in May of that year in Fukayosi, a village in the Bagamoyo district. We finished the research project in October of that year and Ekvall returned to Sweden.

I followed him in late December and in the following months worked tirelessly, seven days a week, to analyze the data and submit the required papers for publication. Fortunately I was allowed to include in my PhD thesis some of the work I had done at BBNP. One of the toughest challenges I faced while writing up my PhD work was what the late twentieth century imposed upon me, as it did on many others. I became, not without some reluctance and reservation, one of the graying generation to venture into the world of the personal computer.

I was given through the research grant a Compaq 386 laptop, which used the MS-DOS command language. In all honesty I have the technical aptitude of the average stem of broccoli, so this was an odyssey that was undertaken with fear and trepidation. It was further complicated by the fact that when I was in school, typing was offered only to those unwilling to try their hands at chemistry and physics. Therefore with great diligence, I have expanded my efforts to the full use of two fingers and partial use of four, using what has been referred to as the biblical system of typing: seek and ye shall find. My supervisor Dr Björkman was as allergic to computers as anyone of his cohort.

Slowly I learned to use my laptop from the manual, which was a nightmare, and in addition I had to learn a statistical package for my data analysis. I must say that ability is a poor man's wealth: I became fairly proficient, and learning the hard way was good, because a skill lasts forever. I no longer fear any digital gadget.

I need to share some experiences from my five-month research with Ekvall in Fukayosi. We stayed in Bagamoyo town and drove every day to Fukayosi. The distance is about thirty-five kilometres but the road was like a highway in hell. We had to cross River Ruvu by a manually operated ferry (we had to pull it by ropes). The ferry operated from six AM to six PM and this daily journey took almost two hours one way.

I will always respect Japanese-made vehicles. We had a robust four-wheel Suzuki Vitara, and it took us religiously daily for five months through the crocodile infested waters of the Ruvu. (Today that road is fully tarmac and there is a bridge across the river.)

One day at our clinic we saw a boy, four years old, with a high fever. His blood slide showed an uncountable number of *Plasmodium falciparum,* what we usually call "stars in the sky." The hemoglobin level was only 4 gm/dl. Clearly the child was very sick and needed blood transfusion and intravenous medication. We decided that since this was not possible at Fukayosi, we should take him to Bagamoyo District Hospital. I told the mother that I would immediately drive the two of them in the faithful Suzuki Vitara and personally treat the child. All this at no cost and I would also pay them for upkeep for all the days of hospitalization. I was convinced that if this child were treated, then within two to three hours the outcome would be positive. But to my disappointment the mother said she had to go home and seek permission from her husband. Her home was another five kilometres from the clinic, so with the mother, myself and a nurse we went to their house. On reaching there we found that the husband was not around, so we waited for two hours until he finally showed up. It was almost three PM and we had to leave before four since the ferry would stop service at six. The husband said I could leave and he would bring the child before nighttime. Reluctantly I left. Earlier, while examining the child, I had told Ekvall that the little boy would surely die. The next day in the morning while crossing the river by ferry we found that the child had indeed died at night because they were unable to cross the river. This was a very painful experience for both of us, and the fact that I had predicted the outcome caused even more distress to Ekvall.

My prediction was based on an understanding of local customs. When we examined the child, he was wearing a chain threaded with old Tanzania coins (which had round holes in their centres) and beads round his waist; there were also scars on the skin around the spleen area, which indicated that the parents had a strong belief in alternative traditional medicine. Before the child was brought to us, the traditional healer had cut the uvula (the teardrop-shaped piece of soft tissue that hangs down the back of the throat), which may have led to blood loss. This was common practice in coastal Tanzania. It was because of these typical signals that I had made my grim prediction; a doctor trained in Sweden would not know about these local practices. I think I was able to convince Ekvall Hakan that I was not a soothsayer or clairvoyant.

Professor Anders Björkman was an excellent supervisor, very humble and always available to help. Apart from what one usually learns in a PhD program, I learned from him how to remain calm during crises and how to be an effective team leader. We became friends and collaborated for many years. In 1998, when Zeenat had developed bilateral nuclear cataracts, he kindly arranged her surgery at one of the best ophthalmic hospitals in Stockholm.

I defended my thesis on December 13, 1996, which is also Saint Lucia's day in Sweden. My PhD thesis was titled *Malaria control measures: Impact on malaria and anaemia in a holoendemic area of rural coastal Tanzania.* My external examiner was Professor Walther H Wernsdorfer from Vienna, a renowned malariologist and author of two authoritative books on malaria. There was also a panel of six professors from the Karolinska Institutet. I was well prepared and at around two PM I was informed that I had passed the PhD examination.

Traditionally, there is always a celebration after a PhD defense. In my case Professor Björkman gave the party at his residence where he invited many colleagues. It was a memorable evening and at some stage I was asked to speak about my experiences in Sweden. With the loss of some sobriety due to the local vodka, I gave perhaps a longer speech than usual, but I recall acknowledging that Sweden was very welcoming and tolerant of different cultural practices. I spoke about its high taxes, but noted that its citizens enjoyed a high quality of life; there was a lot of generosity around and abject poverty was nonexistent. Without any doubt I was very impressed with the Swedish political system of social democracy—a parliamentary constitutional monarchy.

Exhausted and homesick, two days after my defence I returned to Tanzania and was back at Muhimbili.

With a PhD now, I became some sort of a malaria guru. I advised the Ministry of Health on malaria control, and in the era of chloroquine resistance, I was instrumental in conducting research and providing evidence for a need to change the policy on treating the disease. I had two research stations in rural areas where drug-resistance studies were performed.

Chloroquine resistance became a major national issue. While there was overwhelming evidence that the failure rate of the drug was around fifty percent, there was also a lot of hesitancy and refusal to accept this evidence. I was advocating for a change of policy, but we did not have a good alternative candidate. What we had was a temporary measure as we waited for a new drug. It was the consensus that we should now use Sulphadoxine/pyrimethamine (Fansidar). On one occasion, the Minister of Health, who was a veteran physician, came out publicly and said that when he had fever he had taken chloroquine and gotten better, thus there was no resistance. At the ministry and in the malaria control program as well as the National Institute of Medical Research (NIMR), no one would comment on this statement, because their boss was the minister. I contacted a television channel, DTV, and in an interview there I was able to relay the scientific reasons for my viewpoint and gave my opinion that what the Minister of Health was promoting was incorrect.

I cannot understand how an experienced physician could not

understand the concepts of sample size and scientific inference. This Chloroquine vs Fansidar controversy was a hot topic in the corridors of the Ministry of Health, and it reached a peak when at a meeting in Arusha, the Chief Medical Officer accused me of owning a stake in a Fansidar-producing plant and thus I had a vested interest in the distribution of the drug. This was not only untrue but also a political move (it is easy to blame "Asians"), but as we will see later, malaria is also a political disease. I stood my ground, and in 1999 the Ministry of Health changed its policy on the treatment drug.

While all this was going on, I was appointed head of the Department of Parasitology & Medical Entomology, where some years before I had started out as a humble laboratory techni-cian. With increased intake of students (medical, dental, nursing, and pharmacy) the teaching load was heavier, and administrative responsibility greater. Additionally, I was travelling a lot outside Tanzania to attend meetings and conferences. My trips to Geneva, where WHO is based, were very frequent.

I vividly remember my stays at Hotel Moderne in Geneva. My room was always on the seventh floor, because it was cheaper—rooms on the seventh floor were not self-contained. The bathrooms were in the corridor, but I always told my colleagues that I preferred the cheaper room because it had the best view of the lake. I also recall with some amusement now, how once I took a Kenya Airways evening flight to London, attended a meeting till four PM, and returned to Dar on the return flight. It was like visiting a suburb of Dar. I was extremely busy and enjoying every minute of my work.

More teaching and research

I took a much more active teaching role, and at any time I had up to four masters students to supervise. I also supervised PhD students. In 1997, in collaboration with Heidelberg University in Germany, we started a one-year Master of Public Health program, which I was selected to coordinate. To get approval from the University of Dar es Salaam senate proved rather difficult, since masters programs had always been of two years' duration. Finally I gave my own example as a product of the London School of Tropical Medicine with a one-year master's degree. That worked, and the program was approved. Each year the cohort consists of twenty-five to thirty students, and the program is one of the most popular on the campus.

There were many more upward positions to reach; hard work and determination are the keys to success. There is a feeling in the Asian community that because of their race, higher positions are denied to them and reserved only for Black Africans. I believe strongly that this view is false and I am a living example. At no time in my career of more than forty years was I ever discriminated against because of my race or religion. Tanzania is unique in this aspect, and this is due to the father of the nation, Mwalimu Nyerere, who was instrumental in breaking down the barriers of tribalism, skin colour, religion, and ethnicity. If there were a global index of racial tolerance Tanzania would score very high.

Over the years I trained a group of young academicians in the field of malaria research to ensure succession after I retired, and in this effort SIDA/Sarec of Sweden funded us. This funding has lasted until the present. My collaborator was again Professor Anders Björkman. The goal of our project was to improve malaria case management. Over time we trained a number of masters-level students and some PhDs.

One success story involves my undergraduate student Bill Ngasala, who is the current Head of the Department of Parasitology & Medical Entomology. Bill came to my attention when he was a fourth-year medical student and I gave him some temporary work during his vacation. When he finished his medical studies, he joined the National Institute of Medical Research (NIMR) at its Mwanza station, but always stayed in touch with me, because of his interest in malaria research. Through the Swedish research grant, I accepted him as my PhD student. Just like me he enrolled at Karolinska Institutet in Sweden but did all his data collection in Tanzania. He performed remarkably well in his studies and defended his PhD in Stockholm, where I was present. To the surprise of many at my department, I was able to use my network to convince the Director of NIMR to allow Bill to join our faculty. Today I am proud of my association with him. He has taken over from me, as Head of Department and actively involved in malaria research.

Apart from the Swedish malaria research project I also became part of the Muhimbili-Harvard research collaboration sometimes in early 2000. This Muhimbili-Harvard research collaboration had many projects, but my involvement was with how micronutrients impact outcomes in HIV, malaria, tuberculosis, and in pregnancy, and worked in collaboration with Professor Fawzi Wafaie. His passion, hard work, and fairness fitted very well with my own ethic, and we worked closely for over a decade. Through Wafaie's contacts at Harvard I became involved with the Institute for Health Metrics and Evaluation (IHME) in their Global Burden of Disease (GBD) project. The Director of IHME was Dr Christopher J L Murray. Under his leadership IHME has contributed immensely to global public health, and during the coronavirus pandemic its models have been used by President Trump's task force. Their main funding comes from the Bill and Melinda Gates Foundation.

Just after 9/11 in 2001, I arrived at Boston's Logan airport. The aim of my visit was to spend three months at the Harvard School of Public Health, in the department of immunology. My aim was to work in the field of molecular biology and specifically to do polymerase chain reaction (PCR) on blood collected on filter paper. I also had an opportunity to teach in their International Health course for practicing physicians. I taught about malaria, lymphatic filariasis, schistosomiasis, and some other parasitic infections and was asked to set an examination paper on these topics. I made up the questions and submitted them to the course coordinator. To my utter surprise the head of the department called me and said that my questions were too difficult and I should revise them to make them easier for students to answer. Her premise apparently was that a Harvard student should not drop out unless they are highly irresponsible. The questions I had submitted were mostly those I would set for my undergraduate class at Muhimbili. It seemed that the label "Ivy League" was more important than merit. It is status that counts.

Another area I became interested in was the conduct of clinical trials in sub-Saharan Africa. I worked with scientists from the company Novartis, and we performed the first ever clinical trial on Artemether plus Lumefantrine dosage, specifically studying the difference between administering four doses to a patient against six. We found that with six doses there were fewer relapses than with four doses. Today Artemether-Lumefantrine (Coartem) is the first-line medicine for the treatment of malaria in sub-Saharan Africa.

In present-day medical research, clinical trials pose a substantial ethical challenge. Ethics in medical research had become a new passion of mine. I should mention one particularly memorable incident.

I had landed at New Orleans airport but my luggage had not arrived with me. I was attending the annual conference of the American Society of Tropical Medicine. I was promised that my suitcase would be delivered to me at my hotel. On the day of the conference, *The Lancet* came out with results of a new clinical research program. It had been lauded as the "Best Paper of the Year" by this prestigious publication and there was a celebration on the evening of my arrival, to which I went wearing the clothes I had worn during my travel. Later, and even during my flight back, I read that paper over and over. Something did not appear right.

Back at Muhimbili I contacted the Professor of Biostatistics, Karim Hirji, and shared my thoughts on the paper. He took it from me and the next day in an excited mood he came to me and said that he had discovered a number of ethical flaws in the paper. We decided to write a complete critical article on it, and not just a simple rebuttal. Our critique was nineteen pages. Professor Hirji sent it to *The Lancet* but rather intentionally, it seemed to us, the editor took it as a letter and sent it to the main author of the primary paper for comment. This was a breach of ethics in itself, and we were very unhappy about this. We withdrew our paper and sent it to another journal where it was accepted. The main ethical flaws were in the implementation of the research project, mixing of data from three very different sites and data-dragging to prove the research question.

I have had a number of communications with epidemiologists from East Africa and outside, who use it to teach how to critique a scientific paper. The scope of ethics in medical research is very wide and there is a lot to learn on this topic.

Meanwhile I continued with my research interest and was busy with postgraduate students with their research proposals and write-ups. In between I also did research on lymphatic filariasis, which remains a neglected scourge along the coast of East Africa.

Some thoughts about public health challenges in sub-Saharan Africa

It is an unfortunate fact that sub-Saharan African countries face a triple epidemic or burden of diseases. There is the endemicity of tropical infections like malaria, TB, HIV, and some neglected others. Next is the creeping epidemic of noncommunicable diseases

(NCDs). Thirdly, on a periodic basis there arrive fatal epidemics of exotic viruses like Ebola and COVID-19.

There is no way these developing countries can address the growing burden of NCDs. The central important cause of NCDs is insulin resistance, which leads to a metabolic syndrome that comprises increased insulin levels, obesity (mostly with visceral fat deposits), chronic inflammation, hyperglycemia, high blood pressure, abnormal lipid profiles, heart diseases, stroke, vascular diseases, and kidney diseases. These are chronic diseases and their management needs long-term prescriptions of polypharmacy and lifestyle changes. Poor populations cannot afford the costs of most of these medicines and, coupled with ignorance and lack of facilities, there is very little information and willingness about lifestyle changes. So is the continent doomed? No, there are solutions.

Medical research, especially stem-cell research, and DNA technology, are bringing new hopes for the management of NCDs. Instead of life-long dependences on expensive polypharmacy through these new discoveries, permanent cures will become available in the not very distant future. We will be able to cure rather than control these diseases. Africa needs to do three things, first it should not miss the opportunity of stem-cell research in this new era of scientific advance, it should have the appropriate human capacity for it; second, it does not need outside help or financing to come up with programs that address lifestyle changes. Each country can do this, but either there is no such program or it is in the files of the respective Ministries of Health. There are no tangible implementable plans. Third, sub-Saharan African countries need to improve their health systems and health infrastructures. There is a lot of emphasis on mono disease control programs like those for HIV and malaria, and this rather strict compartmentalization coupled with poor health systems and infrastructure is not very efficient.

7

The Five Enigmas of Malaria

You cannot end poverty in Africa without defeating malaria. (Self-observation) Does poverty cause malaria or does malaria cause poverty?

Malaria is a complex protozoal infection caused by parasites of the genus *Plasmodium*. Among them, *Plasmodium falciparum* causes cerebral malaria, which is fatal if untreated. In sub-Saharan Africa this form of malaria is by far the most prevalent. The other three species are *Plasmodium vivax*, *P malariae* and *P ovale*. My career involved mostly *Plasmodium falciparum* (Pf).

The first enigma of malaria is that Pf has a complex life cycle that alternates between the vector, which is the female Anopheline mosquito, and the human. What infects what is a matter of conjecture. Within each host the parasite changes its shape, form, antigenic makeup, and haploid or diploid state (i.e. from one state to the other), and at each of these stages the parasite reproduces both asexually and sexually inside the vector. Because of this complexity, it has survived well and eluded the efforts of vaccine specialists. Even today, the trial vaccine, unlike the polio or smallpox vaccines, has marginal efficacy. We do not have a hundred percent efficacious vaccine.

On the other hand, this complex life cycle exposes the parasite to multiple potential targets of attack. One can destroy the parasite while in the vector or even kill the vector. The parasites enter the bloodstream of the human host during a mosquito bite in elongated forms known as sporozoites. These enter the liver cells and mature into small round schizonts. One schizont can fission into thousands of merozoites (the resultant organisms) that come out of the liver cells and invade the red blood cells (RBC). In the red blood cells the parasite develops further and asexual reproduction continues. At some point the RBC invasion causes symptoms like fever, malaise etc. If this is not diagnosed and treated appropriately severe malaria sets in. Again at some later time the parasites, now in the form of the merozoites, decide to become sexual-stage gametocytes and what really triggers this drastic change remains unknown. The gametocyte will wait to be sucked by the vector (the mosquito) to initiate a sporogonic cycle (i.e. formation of spores containing sporozoites). At each stage the parasite evokes a multitude of immune responses just to confuse the immune system of the host; this is one of the survival strategies deployed by the parasite. There is much that is still unknown in this life cycle, but perhaps by applying the tools of molecular biology some things will become clearer.

The second enigma about malaria is its laboratory diagnosis. A negative result in a blood test does not rule out malaria, especially severe or cerebral malaria, because the parasites sequestrate in the deeper capillaries and are not visualized in peripheral circulation from where the blood for the test is taken. It is very difficult to count the parasites and the existing methodology is inaccurate and may not reflect the actual biomass of the parasite. But to add to this misery the count of the parasite does not guide treatment options nor does it indicate severity. In malaria-endemic countries, children below twelve years who are at school when their blood is examined will have high counts of the parasite but will have no illness. In one of my mobile clinics in Matimbwa village, we took about eighty blood slides and returned in the afternoon to Bagamoyo for staining the slides and checking for parasites. One slide had an uncountable number of parasites. It was just full of them. I decided to go back to the village, expecting that the girl might develop severe malaria. When I saw the nine-year-old, she was busy playing with her mates, jumping rope. I was surprised and also embarrassed; the parents did not understand my concerns. I followed up with the child the next day and her blood slide was positive but the count was decreasing. On the fourth day her blood slide was negative and she was normal—she had gone from an extremely high count to a negative slide and while remaining asymptomatic. This was puzzling. My only explanation, a weak one, is that her immune system had been at work, but I cannot explain how. It is because of this example that the Rapid Diagnostic Test was developed to screen the positives from the negatives, but this is still not the answer to the enigma, because there are about twenty percent of patients who remain positive even post treatment but are asymptomatic. Now the Polymerase Chain Reaction (PCR) technique is used (though not in clinical practice) to pick the lowest parasite biomass, that is, one or two circulating parasites. The dilemma is, should a doctor treat a patient with a positive result but no symptoms, or a patient who shows the disease. If those who are asymptomatic but carry parasites in their blood are not treated, what are the short-term and long term effects on the host's health? Perhaps this is the question I would have liked to address had I not retired. Years later, in 2017 when I was in Nairobi, I did an evaluation for an Israeli company on their new Parasight platform. They had come up with a new machine that in real time could compare the blood of a patient using five million images of malaria parasites, and if there were a match it would indicate positivity. Even with the help of digital technology to improve malaria diagnosis, the dilemma of the doctor remains. The digital platform of diagnosis was equally accurate, with a high degree of sensitivity and specificity; it was easy to perform and took less time.

The third enigma regards the presentation of the disease. There is no pathognomonic symptom or physical sign of malaria. The disease presentation is totally nonspecific and the patient presents with fever or high fever or no fever, malaise, and joint pains which could easily just as well indicate a viral or even bacterial infection. Coupled with the dilemma in laboratory diagnosis, the treatment of such patients becomes difficult and at times nonscientific. Should the patient receive antimalarial treatment, with its harmful side effects? Treating without adequate diagnosis could lead to the development of resistance, which is a major public health problem. Millions of doses of antimalarials are dispensed to millions of patients who perhaps do not need the medication. Currently there is a lot of information coming out of the World Health Organization and other global agencies to the effect that the occurrence of malaria has decreased in sub-Saharan Africa. I agree with such data. Yet no one talks about treatment doses of the drug. It seems that antimalarials are used like candy or peanuts, to be freely ingested at the slightest excuse. I know that even hangovers due to alcohol intake are treated with antimalarials! Such is the enigma of malaria. Let me illustrate this enigma with two examples.

A high-ranking politician in Tanzania rang me from Dodoma, the political capital of the country, to say that he was told by doctors to see me because he had resistant malaria. He had been treated with quinine and Artemether without any improvement, and so he wanted to come and see me. I agreed and saw him in my office, in Dar es Salaam. His main complaint was fever and severe fatigue. I did a rapid malaria test, which was negative, so I took venous blood and gave him Aspirin to relieve the pain and told him to return the next day for the blood results. He was indeed not happy because he expected much more aggressive treatment, but I managed to convince him that we needed to see the blood test results. The next day the test result showed that his uric acid level was elevated to almost five times the normal value. I started the standard gout treatment and in five days he felt much better. There was no need to treat him with antimalarials.

My second case was a female patient referred from Songea (in south Tanzania) who had been treated with quinine and many other antimalarials. Her complaints were mainly fatigue, mild fever, and some depression. I examined her blood slide and it was negative for malaria. Further blood tests indicated a high level of the thyroid stimulating hormone TSH. She had hypothyroidism and treatment with thyroxine ameliorated her symptoms. I met her husband a few days later and he added that her sex drive had also improved. The diagnostic enigma of malaria disease is a big issue especially in poor endemic countries.

The fourth enigma of malaria is how do you predict the outcome of the disease, since there are no indications to say who will develop a severe disease and die or who will recover post treatment with oral antimalarials. At the onset, if there are ten children in an endemic area exposed to uniform conditions, six will have asymptomatic parasitemia of varying parasite biomass. Out of these six perhaps four will develop symptomatic malaria, two will recover with oral treatment, and the other two will develop severe malaria requiring hospitalization and one of them will eventually die. This is the picture on the ground and at every point there are unknowns. Why four children out of the ten in this sample do not develop parasitemia remains unknown. Why two get uncomplicated malaria and are treated and why two develop a severe disease and one dies is also a scientific puzzle. There are no predictable markers. And when a scientific explanation is lacking, it is very difficult to institute intervention measures.

It is well known that immunity plays an important role in all this, but the dynamics and the interactions of the immune system are still unknown. When a tourist enters an endemic area and has no immunity, the disease can be extremely fatal. When I was working at the Dar es Salaam Aga Khan Hospital, one night at around midnight a young man of about twenty-two years and probably from Japan entered the outpatient department. He had high fever and looked very sick. He could not speak English or Kiswahili, thus communication was not easy. It seemed that he had walked into the hospital after seeing the Red Cross sign outside. I immediately started an intravenous line with a dextrose-saline solution and took the blood slide. Before the results were ready, the patient had stopped breathing and died. His blood was full of malaria parasites. I was able to retrieve his passport from his pocket and realized that indeed he was from Japan. I rang the Japanese embassy and this was past midnight but they were very cooperative and within minutes the wife of the ambassador came to the hospital. Later on we came to know that the patient was a tourist who had landed at Kilimanjaro Airport two weeks back and had visited the Ngorongoro as well as the Serengeti national parks. He then took a bus from Arusha and arrived late evening in Dar es Salaam. Most likely he was already feverish and confused and started roaming around the city, and after a few hours entered the hospital. Very likely he was not on any prophylaxis. The point is that for an immunologically naive patient, the disease becomes fatal in a very short time.

In 1992 I was invited to Washington to give a plenary session in a conference about malaria control using insecticide-treated mosquito nets. I had made about twenty transparencies, and on arrival I discovered that the first introductory transparency was missing. The missing transparency depicted the global distribution of malaria. Fortunately the organizers took me to a library and I was able to prepare a new transparency of the global map. My presentation was well received, there were a few questions and the discussions were positive. In that meeting there were many malaria experts, but the global map that I projected was not of malaria distribution per se but of global poverty distribution, which in 1992 was a mirror image of malaria global distribution. No expert in the audience seemed to realize this.

It is a known and easily understandable fact that reducing poverty has an immediate effect on the reduction of malaria incidences. Malaria is a disease of the poor people. It is also a social disease. I always asked this question to my class. What caused malaria in the context of the child who died on the Ruvu river bank, when I visited her with my Swedish colleague? Was it anaemia due to a *Plasmodium falciparum* infection, or was it due to the lack of a bridge across the river, or was it because of gender domination, in that the mother had to get permission from her husband before letting the boy come to the clinic, causing the delay? Was it due to ignorance and blind beliefs in traditional healing? There is no one correct answer; a combination of circumstances was responsible for the mortality. Agriculture practices and development, population movement and unplanned urbanization are some of the factors that have a significant impact on malaria.

8

Malaria Control in Practice

Baseball and malaria keep coming back. Why?

GENE MAUCH

The political factor

Political commitment is important in the control of malaria and it should be realistic, which is definitely difficult in politics. In April 2011, it came as a surprise to me that President Jakaya Kikwete was holding a ceremony at the Leaders Club in Kinondoni, with the theme Kick Out Malaria by 2015. This was totally unrealistic and perhaps a political gimmick. I guessed that the president had received advice from expatriate agencies, who at that time were working in the National Malaria Control Program. As a local expert I should have been consulted. A few days before, at a meeting, this slogan was discussed and I opposed it on scientific grounds. It was just not possible at that time to "kick out malaria by 2015," and clearly the president was ill advised. Since the deployment of insecticide-treated bed nets (ITBNs), it has become fashionable for politicians, especially close to election time, to be seen in the media distributing bed nets to pregnant women and children. Only for the purpose of scoring political points.

I feel strongly that in malaria-endemic areas using a bed net is not a privilege but a right. However, from a scientific viewpoint, bed nets can only reduce transmission if the coverage, that is it's utilization is over ninety percent. If the coverage is less, it protects the individual but is not a public-health tool. There is a lot of misinformation that the current dip in malaria prevalence is due to ITBNs. Use of bed nets certainly has contributed to some reduction, but the overall reduction is mainly due to the use of combination therapy (Artemether+Lumefantrine) as first-line medication. For the first time in the history of malaria control the chosen medication is also gametocidal. This means that in the human host when the parasite (merozoite) decides to change its form to a sexual stage, awaiting to infect the mosquito (mosquitoes should suck blood in order to propagate themselves), this sexual stage is rendered nonviable by this medication. Thus it is now lowering transmission.

Chloroquine did not have this property, it was only killing the asexual stages in the blood and liver, which are responsible for typical malaria symptoms. Fansidar on the other hand is well known to promote gametogenesis thereby *increasing* malaria transmission. Fansidar is a combination of Sulphadoxine and pyrimethamine, and it was used sporadically during the Chloroquine era. In the mid 1990s, when resistance to chloroquine was at its peak Fansidar was recommended as a replacement medication on a temporary basis while there was ongoing research for new molecules to treat malaria.

All these facts are experimentally proven. ITBNs are a good tool for politicians to pursue their political goals.

Another effective tool for combating malaria is to spray outdoors and indoors with insecticide. The timing of the spraying is an important factor and politicians can easily manipulate it. During a campaign period, why not show the population that something tangible is being done to reduce mosquitoes? I have had to deal with this phenomenon during a Japanese campaign to control mosquitoes in urban Dar es Salaam.

In 1998 Tanzania had excess rainfall in the April-May rainy season. These rains, referred to as the El Nino rains, precipitated an epidemic of malaria, especially in northwestern Tanzania around Lake Victoria. The roads were cut off due to floods and medical supplies were delayed. The minister of health, Dr Aron Chiduo, asked me to go to Bukoba and Muleba to assess the impact of the rains on malaria in the region and to report back within a week. I flew to Bukoba via Mwanza with some medical supplies. The main prison in Bukoba Township had an outbreak of cholera and I was told to stop there and see if they needed any assistance from the ministry. On arrival in Bukoba I went straight to the Regional Medical Officer (he had been informed about my visit), and we went immediately to the prison.

This was the first time I saw the inside of a prison. I spent about five hours there trying to establish a system to control the outbreak. The isolation of patients was already in place but it was inadequately managed. The prison doctor was a medical assistant, who himself was serving a sentence in the jail. I worked with him to put in place stringent rules about who entered the isolation ward. At the entry and exit doors there was an antiseptic solution, and protocols for washing the linen and disposal of excreta were created. All prisoners and the prison police were given Tetracycline as prophylaxis. A week later, when I was leaving Bukoba, I met the head of the medical prisons in the country. We knew each other from our days at Muhimbili and he said to me that I had done a good job in Bukoba and that within a week of my visit the prison outbreak had been controlled.

While in Bukoba I also visited the pediatric ward of the Regional

Hospital and could not believe what I saw there. Every space was utilized to accommodate a child and every child was receiving a blood transfusion and intravenous quinine. It was total chaos because the staff were overwhelmed. What was done to manage the severe malaria was correct. A decade of Chloroquine resistance resulted in inadequate clearance of parasitaemia, the persistence of which caused malarial anaemia. Due to excess rainfall and collection of water bodies the mosquito vector flourished and multiplied leading to upsurge cases of severe malaria and life-threatening malarial anemia. In a few patients I checked the dosage of intravenous quinine prescribed and this was accurate. There was nothing much I could have done given the circumstances of this sudden increase of severe malaria. My takeaway lesson from this experience was that in-service training for frontline workers is very essential.

Next I drove to Muleba district, some seventy kilometres south of Bukoba. It took us three hours due to the condition of the road. Muleba district had a government health centre in front of the town centre and there was also a designated district hospital, Rubya, run by the Catholic Church. At the health centre the situation was truly bad. There were no diagnostic facilities, and under-five mortality had almost quadrupled. I had to spontaneously teach the staff how to manage severe malaria and with the meager supply that I had brought we were able to start treatment with intravenous quinine, though the much-needed blood transfusions could not be given.

Next we went to the designated Rubya district hospital and there were patients everywhere. During that visit I met the local member of parliament, a young lawyer at that time, who is currently Tanzania's ambassador to the United States. He was forceful; he had raised the issue in parliament, which was why I had been ordered to perform an evaluation of the situation. He wanted to take me around in his constituency to show his voters that he had brought an expert from Muhimbili. This was to gain political points. But the district medical officer wanted to take me around to see what the real issues were. Between these two, I played a very diplomatic act and at the end of my visit I think they were both happy.

Back in Bukoba I spent a night at a place called Banana Inn. While I was seated outdoors, a pipe-smoking gentleman came to my table. I was also a pipe smoker in those days. I at once recognized him as the minister of labour and youth and MP for rural Bukoba. He wanted to take me around the next morning to see the devastation in his constituency. I was in a dilemma, since I was flying out the next morning to Dar es Salaam and later that night taking a KLM flight to Geneva via Amsterdam. If I agreed to his request, I would miss my trip to Geneva. With his position and influence he could have very easily stopped me from departing Bukoba, and there was only one flight per day. I was in a very difficult situation and very politely explained to him that I had seen the problem in his region and my report to the ministry would recommend urgent action. He was not happy about this, but I also told him that I had spoken to the minister of health. This was not true but he accepted that. Later in early 2000 we became friends, because I treated one of his family members who had intestinal myiasis, something not very common. We even exchanged pipe tobacco from time to time.

Politicians do have a big role to play in supporting public health issues. But it has to be done with honesty, which is a rare commodity in politics.

My next encounter with a prison was when I was back from Geneva. My office in those days was at the Central Pathology Laboratory of Muhimbili Hospital. There were four prisoners waiting on the main floor for their blood slide results. This was rather surprising, because the prison in Ukonga, in Dar es Salaam, had a well-equipped medical clinic. The next day I saw ten prisoners waiting for their results. I asked the technician what was going on. He said the men were referred from Ukonga prison to rule out malaria. Blood slides were done and the results from the Muhimbilii laboratory showed that the blood slides were all negative. I took a slide to re-examine under the microscope and surprisingly saw the spirochete, Borrelia recurrentis, which causes louse-borne relapsing fever (LBRF). These men were not suffering from malaria but LBRF. I then contacted the chief prison medical officer based in Dar es Salaam, my friend whom I had met in Bukoba just weeks back, and told him the diagnosis. LBRF can easily be treated with either penicillin or tetracycline, but I wanted to visit the Ukonga prison to observe the transmission pattern. He arranged this and when I visited the prison, I asked to see where the prisoners slept. I was taken there and under one blanket I saw millions of lice. I instructed the authorities that all clothing be washed in boiling water and the entire prison be fumigated. Washing clothes in boiling water was not a problem, but fumigation needed permission from the Chief Prisons Officer. I believe it was done later. A few days later I wrote about this interesting occurrence in order to publish my findings, but my friend the medical officer said that that was strictly not allowed.

9

Time and Tide

The two most powerful warriors are patience and time.

LEO TOLSTOY, *War and Peace*

Time had passed too quickly since I joined Muhimbili University of Health and Allied Sciences as a medical student, and although it was more than ten years since my marriage, it seemed that I had married only recently. In that time I had achieved a certain status in my field of malaria and parasitic infections. My son Zainil was a teenager and was about to start university. We had lost my mother-in-law while I was studying in Stockholm. So now we were only four, Zeenat, Zainil, my mother, and myself. I lost my mother on December 31, 1999; she was 93 years old and missed the new century by a day.

In September 1998 it was time to say farewell to Zainil. He had been accepted at the University of Calgary as an international student to pursue an undergraduate degree in Actuarial Science. I had no idea what this involved, but he clarified and I was surprised: how could he pursue a degree that needed pure and applied mathematics while in high school he had taken biology? Officially he also did math as a subsidiary subject but, later I discovered that he had been pursuing pure and applied mathematics in his free time.

My desire had been to make him a doctor, to follow in my foot-steps, and he had agreed. I have no regret that he followed his own mind and interest because he is successful and enjoying his work. While he was studying in Calgary we once had a conversation about mathematics and statistics, and he convinced me how power-ful they can be. Since then I have been inspired to at least upgrade my knowledge of biostatistics.

His departure made me very sad because I had a feeling that maybe we should have spent more time together. Our relation-ship now was more a friendship, and we played a lot of badminton together. After his departure I found myself increasingly spend-ing more time at home with my wife. For the first time, in 2002, we took a holiday while the university students were on strike, and we went to India for five weeks. It was indeed memorable. Though India is my ancestral home, I did not know anybody there, nor was I intending to find my roots. For me it was a holiday to enjoy and see India. I must say that this was a short rather unplanned vaca-tion, and I feel that maybe India refuses to be described in brief. Nevertheless I will attempt to reflect upon my perception of India. We landed at Mumbai airport in the morning and it took us two hours to clear immigration and customs. I knew the hotel we would stay at—Sagar Hotel in Byculla had been recommended by friends in Dar es Salaam. We took a taxi to the hotel and fortunately we got a room at 1400 Indian rupees per night. After the long overnight flight we were tired and needed to rest. Later in the evening it was time to roam around the hotel and I was in for a big surprise. It was the holy month of Ramadan, and it was time to end the fast and all the streets were full of people. I had not seen such a big crowd; even walking was difficult. I was afraid that we might get separated, and so I tied my hand with Zeenat's with a handkerchief and we walked in the nearby streets. Truly India is a place to see, hear, feel, taste, and smell things you may have never sensed in your life, both perplexing and pleasing. My first impression was there is no shortage of people in India. This overpopulation brings opportunities, but paradoxically there was also no shortage of poverty and smelly slums. India was loud and crowded and there were days when walking down the street amazed me, and days when it overwhelmed me. Sometimes the autorickshaw drivers weaved in and out of traffic so recklessly that I would gasp audibly. Despite the chaos and turmoil there is some order and people survive and many are happy. I wonder about the visitors who come to India searching for inner peace in the midst of frenzy and pandemonium. Beggars are relentless, and my heart was breaking seeing small children begging professionally.

There was one particularly sweet girl of about five or six years who came frequently to beg. Zeenat was heart-broken and she would give the girl a loaf of bread instead of rupees. We met her parents, who were staying in a cardboard shed around the light post outside the hotel. Zeenat felt so much empathy with her that she offered to adopt her. The offer was to take the girl with us to Tanzania and educate her, and when she finished her education she could return to her parents. It was futile, as expected; the parents refused flatly. Later we bought new clothes and took the girl to our hotel room, gave her a bath, and dressed her. A few hours later she was again dirty and her hair was undone. The hotel staff told us that it was part of their training to beg.

I had decided to survive on a stringent budget so we were mostly using public transport or walking. Once we walked from the famous Juhu beach back to Sagar Hotel, and it took us almost five hours. The hotel staff were all amazed. We also depended mostly on street food, and luckily we never had health problems. Street food is safe because it is freshly cooked.

After a few days in Mumbai we took the Rajdhani Express to New Delhi. We arrived at New Delhi railway station at around ten AM and took a three-wheeler to search for a hotel. One lesson I learned in India was to never agree to stay in a hotel based on the splendour of the reception area, but always to check the rooms first. We took a day tour of New Delhi and later a tourist bus to Agra to see the Taj Mahal. A moment that I will never forget was at sunset when the sky over the Taj Mahal was orange with shades of rose. In the midst of so much power and beauty, I felt more romantic, sensual, and fragile than I ever had before. No words can adequately describe that experience.

We returned to Mumbai and visited Mahabaleshwar hill stations, Goa, and Pune. In Pune we visited the Aga Khan bungalow, which is now a museum dedicated to Mahatma Gandhi. We started walking back to the central station but it started raining, so to escape getting wet we entered a cinema on the way. The movie turned out to be about the life of Dr Ambedkar, and since then I have read a lot about this popular activist.

Exactly after five weeks vacationing in India, we left Mumbai for Dar es Salaam. Apart from overpopulation and poverty, my other concerning observation about India was the high level of air and water pollution. I was also saddened and disappointed by how India was managed politically, socially, and economically.

Back in Dar es Salaam, in 1998 I was able to send my son to study in Calgary. This was a tough decision, and initially Zeenat was hesitant to send our only child so far away. However, Zainil had chosen actuarial science as his subject, and it was not available at local universities. Considering the salaries in Tanzania in dollars, the choice was by no means cheap, but I was in a much better financial position now. Coming out of the vicious cycle of poverty is a process and perhaps I was now seeing some financial comfort. When I reflect today about our decision, I feel proud that we made the right decisions in letting our son pursue his interests abroad.

Zainil visited Tanzania for two weeks when he completed his third year. While in Dar es Salaam we explored opportunities for employment for an actuary. Unfortunately the private sector was still in its infancy, not as it is today, and there were no jobs for him. We decided it was in his best interest to remain in Canada, look for a suitable job and if possible to enroll in a master's program. Zainil completed his studies and found a job in Calgary, and ever since he has been performing well. Again reflecting on this decision, do I feel guilty that my son decided to remain in Canada and not return to Tanzania? All his education from primary onwards was paid by us and he never received any help from the government nor from any other institution, so he was ethically and morally not bound to return to Tanzania. I have a feeling that he is in a much better situation now to serve his country of birth and maybe once his children start university he may decide to relocate to Tanzania, although the current policy of the government does not encourage diaspora status.

In 2007 he rang me and said he wanted to get married to his sweetheart, Reeshma, his girlfriend from Tanzania. The marriage took place in Edmonton, so Zeenat and I went to Calgary and then on to attend the wedding. It was a perfect wedding; my short and simple advice to my son was, your wife is someone's daughter, someone's sister, so if you ever in any way abuse her that will be a reflection of my failure in your upbringing.

Reeshma, our daughter-in-law, has been the most wonderful miracle in our life. Since I never had a daughter she has very smoothly filled that gap. We have a very deep understanding and she is aware that I am always by her side in case of a need and this feeling is reciprocal. Simple, humble, and caring, she's an amazing mother to our grandchildren. In our family, perhaps due to my own upbringing, we never had a tradition of celebrating birthdays or exchanging gifts, but when Reeshma came she started this tradition and today we celebrate all our birthdays by cutting a cake and giving gifts. Such occasions have the profound effect of unifying a family.

For me, the first decade of the twenty-first century was professionally very fulfilling. I was always on the move and engrossed in teaching and research. But I was either ignoring or denying the fact that slowly the metabolic changes due to age were creeping in. In 2009 I was diagnosed with type 2 diabetes. Today my daily struggle is to get my blood sugar level below 6 mmol/l. At that time in Tanzania we still went to a tailor to have our clothes made; I was wearing tailor-made trousers and even my wedding suit was made by a tailor. When he measured my waist last, he told me jokingly that when the waistline is bigger than the chest, be assured that diabetes, hypertension, and cardiac diseases are around the corner. That observation turned out to be true.

In May 2013 I received the expected letter from our human resource department about my retirement. It was good to know that I was now sixty years old and had reached the peak of my incompetency. I was not caught unprepared, but deep inside, I was convinced that it was not the right thing to retire a professor at sixty when he or she is healthy. It's not that Tanzania has a glut of qualified people. The sixty-year time limit was set many years ago when life expectancy was low.

Be that as it may, in retirement I started publishing articles in *The Citizen*, one of our dailies, on a weekly basis. My column was known as "Thinking Aloud." I wrote once about my view on retirement at sixty. Soon after, the government passed a new law increasing the retirement age of academicians to sixty-five with an opportunity of contract work till seventy. A few colleagues wrote to me to say that they were unhappy about this, because now their retirement benefits would be delayed by five years. Still, many others supported me on this issue.

I had the option to continue at Muhimbili Hospital (MUHAS), but under a contract. However, I had observed a growing nepotism (favouring family and tribal members) at the place. Also, a huge project (funded by a grant from the Bill & Melinda Gates Foundation) was under way to change the curriculum. But in reality, there was simply a rewriting of the same old curriculum using buzzwords. In essence there was no difference in the contents of the courses or the teaching methodology. If anything, the medical training was undergoing dilution by making it much easier to pass the examinations. This was all about how to use and reap project funds.

Apart from the creeping nepotism, there was something else that I did not totally agree with. MUHAS received a huge grant from South Korea to build a tertiary teaching hospital. In a very autocratic decision-making process, a plot was sought some thirty kilometres away near Kibaha on the main Morogoro highway for the new hospital. I could sense opportunism and job-creation at work. Mlongazila Hospital is now functional and is state-of-the-art. I do not think there is any comparable hospital in the country. It started off under the administration of MUHAS, but a university is meant for teaching and not administering a hospital. In my newspaper column I wrote about this problem, and the government decided to move the administration to Muhimbili National Hospital (MNH). But with wider discussions beforehand, this new hospital could have been built next to the MNH, and its utility would have been much higher. With the above misgivings I did not take the offered contract and sought new pastures elsewhere.

10

Tanzanian Politics

Apart from poverty, ignorance and disease the fourth enemy of the people is corruption.

MWALIMU JULIUS NYERERE

Every Tanzanian is passionate about these two things: first, the country's politics, and second, supporting either the Simba or the Young Africans soccer clubs. I kept abreast of local politics. Politicians would sometimes come to see me about health issues, but I intentionally kept them at a distance. I was close to politics but at a safe distance from politicians. I was well informed of what was happening in the country. This helped me a lot later, when I started writing my newspaper column from Calgary.

I grew up during the one-party system of government and the ideology was socialism. There was something unique about it, because it was African socialism, or Ujamaa. If today I hold four degrees and am relatively successful, it is because of Ujamaa. My parents had no means to send me to school.

Our first president and father of the nation, Mwalimu Nyerere, unified the country and the people were largely happy. Importantly, there was dignity, and the gap between the poor and the rich was still acceptable. Systems were put in place to check the rich so they had little room to get richer by sucking (kunyonya, as it was called) the poor. The Ujamaa ideology was based on a historical blueprint known as the Arusha Declaration (Azimio la Arusha). However, many blame the economic decline of the nation to this ideology.

Sometime in 1978 Tanzania was forced into a useless war with Idi Amin of Uganda. I say "useless," because Tanzania did not gain anything and the main cause was that Idi Amin's army, unprovoked, had entered the northern border and started looting and harassing the people. Idi Amin justified this act and actually claimed a part of Tanzania as belonging to Uganda. Unfortunately at that time wisdom did not come forth from any African or global institutions like the United Nations. Nyerere's lifetime dream ended with this senseless war. Perhaps in a bigger picture some global superpowers had intentionally imposed the war to end Tanzania's unique social experiment.

The result of the war is well known; economically we went back years. It was the war and not the Ujamaa ideology that saw Tanzania in a difficult economic situation in the early eighties.

Thus, in the mid-eighties Mwalimu Nyerere voluntarily stepped down, the first African president to do so and with dignity. He could easily have continued, but he decided otherwise. That's when we started the second phase of the presidency of Tanzania. Currently we are in the fifth phase.

When Mwalimu stepped down, he did something very praise-worthy. Though he had been president for twenty-three years, he put in place a law that limited future presidential terms to a maximum of ten years, with elections after the first five years. Fortunately this law has been respected so far.

In the second phase, a multiparty system was introduced, so that the concept of an opposition party started. But until now the government has not changed hands, no opposition party has won an election. Does this mean that democracy is compromised? Or is the opposition weak and too fragmented? I have no answer.

I strongly submit that the greatest enemy of Tanzania and Africa is corruption; the secondary enemies are poverty, disease, and ignorance. Corruption has been the primary cause of poverty. Tanzania is poor despite having an abundance of natural resources and the blame should go towards corruption and the subsequent phases of leadership. All the phases post-Mwalimu did well to maintain peace, harmony, and the strength of the national language, Kiswahili. Through free market policies the economy improved, but cosmetically. Each phase failed to collect revenue to its maximum potential, thus social services were compromised both qualitatively and quantitatively.

Large-scale corruption became the norm, big scams worth billions of dollars involving leaders became fairly common. All this happened because the Ujamaa blueprint, the Arusha Declaration, was conveniently and totally forgotten and collecting dust in the few shelves of the offices. In the ensuing thirty years a new strata of Tanzanians emerged, which became highly addicted to indiscipline and accumulating wealth through corruption. The once narrow gap between the poor and the rich became much wider than could exist even in a super capitalistic state.

One day a prominent wealthy businessman consulted me for health reasons. At some point we started discussing politics, as any devoted Tanzanian would. According to him, in the first phase of the presidency, the responsible minister would listen to you and if needed take you to see the president. In the subsequent phases over the years, the businessman would take the responsible minister to see the president. Leadership became a curse (for the minister) rather than an asset.

Now we are in the fifth phase, under President Magufuli, and things have started to change. Revenue collection has improved significantly. Huge development projects have started and the impact will be felt in the future. There is improvement in the social services, and work-related discipline has improved. However, every Tanzanian complains of economic hardship. But why? To detoxify an addiction is a painful process, especially in the short term. In the long term the benefits will be noticeable and felt by the majority. This detoxification process is a necessary step for future prosperity.

There could be some validity to accusations that the business environment is not enabling. Big-time corruption has definitely been dented but corruption is still rampant, and it appears that there is fatigue in the anticorruption drive. There is a need therefore to reinvigorate the fight against corruption, otherwise the gains that have been made will be unsustainable. There is also a general feeling both within the country and by outsiders that democracy in Tanzania is being constricted and this may be a dangerous trend.

Democracy cannot work the same way in all societies. Its practice must be based on local conditions, culture, and level of development. Without understanding or accepting this, any conclusions about Tanzanian democracy are questionable. Still, there is little doubt that democracy in Tanzania is much less today than it was in the fourth phase administration under President Kikwete. In today's globalized world, rigidity may lead to isolation, and Tanzania will not be able to endure this. Democracy should therefore be protected, and people should elect their leaders based upon good governance.

Tanzania is developing; there is light at the end of the tunnel. The fifth-phase government has finally stopped the decades-long belief that foreign aid can generate sustained economic growth. It is encouraging to see that a number of large infrastructure projects are underway with internally generated funds. I submit today that it is possible to have an aid-free Tanzania. The economy is actually improving, mega corruption is hardly seen, and there is increased local entrepreneurship. There are more opportunities for young people than when I was growing up.

At present, all this seems to be driven by one person, President Magufuli; but in five more years he will have to step down. What one would like to see meanwhile is the strengthening of institutions. At the core of development is accountability. My greatest concern is that despite fewer big corruption scandals, there is still a significant amount of corruption present. In a compromised democracy there can be a serious lack of transparency, where corruption can thrive.

Tanzania is no longer a crying country. Poverty, corruption, disease, lack of infrastructure, the erratic (but mainly poor) economic showing—all these are present across most nations of the African continent. They are the issues that policymakers and governments grapple with each and every day in poverty-stricken countries. What has been unique about Tanzania is its political stability and peaceful nature, unlike the historical propensity for violent unrest and civil wars in the countries of sub-Saharan Africa. This prevailing peace across the country has nurtured the economic growth we see today.

At the 2001 Labour Party conference in Britain, the prime minister of the time, Tony Blair, remarked that "The state of Africa is a scar on the conscience of the world," and the West should provide more aid. This is just another serious misdiagnosis of the African predicament. We do not need aid, we need to be treated fairly economically, and let the richer nations not promote corruption and civil unrest in our societies. We can and we will develop.

The October 2020 national elections in Tanzania

While this book was in the process of publication, national elections took place in Tanzania (October 28, 2020). The ruling party (CCM) once again won the election, this time by an overwhelming majority.

The incumbent president received eighty-four percent of the votes and in parliament only one member of parliament came from the opposition. In the previous parliament there were thirty-plus opposition members. This will be a one-party feast, but the people have spoken. Whether this election was free and fair is a matter of conjecture, but no election can be hundred percent perfect, and as a norm in Africa the opposition will always contest the outcome.

The ruling party was contesting from a unique position. In the past five years (2015-2020), CCM performed what it had promised, something that happened after almost thirty years. People witnessed tangible outcomes and for the first time elections were funded internally. In its campaign, the ruling party was loud about its achievements, and presented a good election manifesto, stating what to expect in the next five years. The opposition put too much emphasis on freedom, justice, and inclusive development. These three points were repeated constantly at the expense of voter boredom and fatigue. Tanzania is not a kleptocracy nor a plutocracy, it has its own democracy that should be given time to grow.

It is important, however, for the ruling party to learn the correct lessons from these elections. For one thing, the constitution of Tanzania should be modified. Too much power is vested in the office of the president, which can be disastrous, because in the future the sitting president could legally become a dictator. Also, Tanzania should promote political freedom and develop democracy beyond the electoral process. There is a need to infuse new thinking about the future, new perceptions of the contemporary world as a multipolar, multicultural, and interconnected entity.

The Covid-19 pandemic in Tanzania

This book would remain incomplete if I do not write about Covid-19 and Tanzania. Public health and disease are my specialty. Perhaps

Tanzania is the only country in the world that has officially declared itself free of Covid-19. In early 2020, I lost a very close friend due to Covid-19 in Dar es Salaam. In late March the president of Tanzania through the Ministry of Health did an anonymous testing of specimens taken from animals like goats and fruits such as pawpaw. The results for COVID-19 turned out to be positive, and this news went viral. There were many humorous clips about this phenomenon. What happened next is that the president urged the nation to pray for three days and then declared Tanzania as free of Covid-19. There is no ongoing testing, face masks are not mandatory, and there is no social distancing; most important, there have been no lockdowns and everyone goes about his or her business. I think what the president did was to treat fear and panic.

The whole world has somehow fallen into a fear and panic trap. There is no example of economic lockdowns in world history, this is the first time we are witnessing lockdowns, and they are proving more detrimental than Covid-19. Fear, panic, anxiety, nervousness, and public hysteria have turned us irrational. I do not dispute the reality of Covid-19; but it is just another bad flu that we need to cope with using intelligence and genuine science.

In basic statistics, students are taught that absolute numbers or data is useless for inference and decision-making; one has to use proportions and rates so that comparisons can be made. Unfortunately, switching your TV and global platforms from renowned universities will display absolute numbers of people infected and deaths, by country. This makes no sense. For any disease outbreak, it is important to present data in terms of incidence, prevalence, and mortality rates, and this requires an agreed upon denominator. This has been totally lacking, and the media consistently exaggerate and politicians become super-scientists. Let me repeat, I am not denying that the coronavirus exists. Covid-19 exists in Tanzania but not fear and panic. The hallmark of the modern world is democracy, but no country sought a referendum from its people on an issue of such magnitude as a complete lockdown. In years to come, history will judge if our actions were intellectually appropriate or not. It would seem that democracy is an illusion, or how could the Western democracies impose dictatorial lockdowns, in which all that was required of individuals was obedience?

11

My Experiences at a Private Medical University in Kenya

Appearances to the mind are of four kinds;
a. Things either are, as they appear to be
b. Or they neither are nor appear to be
c. Or they are, and do not appear to be
d. Or they are not yet appear to be
Rightly to aim in all these cases is the wise man's task

EPICTETUS

In early 2013, in Dar es Salaam, I met the director of research at the Aga Khan University; he was based in Karachi and had received my contact information from a colleague in Nairobi. We talked in general terms about medical research and education. Apparently he was impressed with what I was doing and asked me if I was interested in joining the Aga Khan University Hospital in Nairobi (AKUHN) as Chair of Pathology. The position was vacant and they were searching for a potential candidate.

As I mentioned earlier I belong to the Ismaili community, of which the Aga Khan is the forty-ninth Imam (spiritual leader). I am a devoted follower and practice my faith to my utmost ability. Thus there is an inner call in me to work and contribute to the noble endeavours of the Imam in developing countries. The history of such ethical endeavours spans some three generations in Africa.

As directed, I applied for the position and sometime in January I met briefly with the CEO and the Dean of AKUHN at Serena Hotel in Dar es Salaam. This was a courtesy meeting; they were there for some other purpose but decided to meet me to put a face to my application. I was told that they would call me for an interview in Nairobi latest by end of March, because they wanted the process of hiring to end before the impending national elections in Kenya. Indeed I received a call for the interview, which would be a two-day process and I was also instructed to do a presentation to the faculty about my vision and how I would contribute to the AKUHN.

The Aga Khan University, under the aegis of AKDN, has campuses in Africa and Asia, of which the Aga Khan University Hospital in Nairobi is one. On the website of AKDN is a document describing the guiding principles of AKDN. My observations and experiences that follow here will be in reference to this document, which I consider an important reflection of the aims and inspirations of the Imam for AKDN.

The presence of Aga Khan institutions like schools, hospitals, financial institutions, housing schemes, hotels, industries, and media have a long history in the East African countries. AKUHN in Nairobi started as a dispensary and later was expanded into the Platinum Jubilee Hospital. This hospital was transformed into a university hospital, AKUHN, a few decades back. All these institutions are well established and well functioning and provide quality services. They are among the few private non-government organizations that have been in existence for a long period, surviving in the most adverse of times. This reflects the commitment of the Imam. Despite the lack of financial transparency, AKDN is perhaps the only private institution that to some extent reinvests its profits to further develop itself. This is why the Imam commands a lot of respect internationally as well as in each country where the AKDN is present.

However, during my three years working at AKUHN, my observations and experiences were somewhat different from my expectations. Unfortunately, I found that the environment at AKUHN was not conducive to any sort of discussion. When I resigned, the president of AKUHN phoned me and expressed an interest to meet me. He said his secretary would set up a meeting in Nairobi; however after waiting for seven days without any indication of such a meeting, I wrote an email to him to which he replied that he was no longer in Nairobi. A few days later I received a phone call from his secretary in Karachi to say that he would wish to talk to me over the phone. I politely declined, because I wanted a face-to-face meeting as previously agreed.

My aim here is not to criticize but to bring forward an honest and constructive critique. I'll start with my first interview in Nairobi.

The interview was well structured and on the first day I had to meet with chairs of each department and different leaders in management. The next day I made my presentation, which was well attended. I also took time to talk to faculty and postgraduate students pursuing the master's degree in medicine (MMed).

In one interview, two non-medical experts, the Chief Operating Officer and the Chief Accountant, asked me how I would control hospital-acquired infections. Initially I thought I could easily confuse them by asking whether they meant gram-positive or gram-negative bacteria, these being the two broad classifications of bacteria, as spore formers and non-spore formers. But I decided against that and very politely went through the standard protocol. It seemed they were satisfied but to date I have not understood clearly why someone from the finance department should ask an infectious disease expert about infection control.

Back on the flight to Dar es Salaam I started a thoughtful analysis of the trip. One common question asked by all was how I would make money for the hospital. No one was interested in my teaching or research experience. I was from a public institution and had no idea about how to make money. My experience with monies was limited to managing research project funds. It seemed odd; was I joining a medical academic institution or a financial institution? Since my interview went well and I was informed that they were interested in hiring me, I brushed off these anomalous thoughts and after discussions about salary and other benefits I agreed to join AKUHN starting July 1, 2013.

As per my contract I was to report to the dean for all academic matters and to the CEO or anyone else appointed by him or her for matters related to laboratory management. To my surprise the CEO informed me that I had to report to the Chief Nursing Officer (CNO) for all matters pertaining to laboratory management. I did not understand this: why should I report to a nurse, especially when she had very little knowledge about the laboratory? I had not seen or heard of a head of pathology reporting to a CNO. I initially perceived this as either an example of nepotism or the incompetency of the CEO. Later on it became apparent that the CNO was the de facto CEO and exercising powers beyond her qualifications and knowledge. This unique and weird administrative arrangement fueled a lot of damaging corporate toxicity.

In a discussion regarding the development of the laboratory, one microbiology faculty member informed me that in East Africa there was only one laboratory, which was in Uganda, that did TB drug-resistance testing. Apparently due to HIV, TB infections have flared up in East Africa.

Tuberculosis and HIV/AIDS constitute the main burden of infectious disease in resource-limited countries. In the individual host, the two pathogens, *Mycobacterium tuberculosis* and HIV, potentiate each other, accelerating the deterioration of immunological functions and resulting in premature death if untreated. In this co-infection, the diagnosis of tuberculosis poses a major challenge.

Discussing this with my colleagues in the Department of Pathology, we decided that we should introduce this testing in Nairobi. The demand for it was definitely high. It entailed training two technicians for one to two months in a laboratory where the testing was being done and getting the required equipment. Karachi has a sister teaching hospital, so I rang my counterpart at Aga Khan University Hospital in Karachi and she was very willing to train two of my technicians for two months and give us the needed equipment at no cost. To me this was an excellent opportunity. I had the budget for the technicians' tickets and their upkeep in Karachi. But to finalize the arrangement I had to seek approval from my nurse boss. She rudely and vehemently refused to discuss it, threw my application into the dustbin, and warned me not to interfere with the laboratory administration or to entertain any such matters. I was stunned. I could not understand such deplorable behaviour; it was unacceptable, but I knew of no recourse, since I was still new to the institution. The TB drug-resistance testing idea just ended.

While this happened the CEO, my nurse boss, one faculty from pathology, and I had a meeting. The agenda was quality control of outreach clinics. AKUHN had established about thirty small clinics in the suburbs of Nairobi. Some of these clinics had small laboratories, therefore quality control was necessary. The main hospital had a Joint Commission International (JCI) accreditation, while the outreach clinics had no such accreditation. There was a separate director for the outreach clinics. I was not aware that the outreach clinic laboratories were directly under my supervision. This ignorance infuriated the CEO and perhaps just to impose her authority she started ranting and left the meeting room for a few minutes to regain her composure.

I never understood this tantrum. Any further discussions were compromised, and in an emotional state she directed that I should do whatever possible to look into the quality control program of the laboratories and report monthly to the Chief Accountant (who in my interview had asked me about infection control). Imagine, the Chair of Pathology reporting about the quality control of a laboratory to a graduate of commerce and bookkeeping. My pride and dignity were definitely dented, but more than that I was disturbed by the lack of common sense and leadership and the corporate toxicity at the place.

In three years I was able to upgrade most of these suburban laboratories using the WHO protocol of accreditation at no cost. I did this because I believe that an answer to frenzy and ranting is only action and not to reply in kind. This was my first regret at joining AKUHN and a kind welcome to corporate toxicity. The laboratory staff, the technicians, reception workers, and cleaners all worked in fear.

Once I walked into the laboratory at three AM and saw that the reception staff were seated and had covered themselves with laboratory coats (it gets chilly in Nairobi at night); obviously they were snoozing. I quietly moved around and without disturbing anyone saw the same in different sections. Finally I met one member of staff who was cleaning the floor. I asked her about any pending workload, and she said all the received specimens were analyzed, the results had been posted in the information system, and the ward rounds would restart at five AM. This to me was logical and I quietly left without disturbing anyone.

The next two days the staff were full of anxiety and I could sense some uneasiness and whispers in the corridor. When I inquired, the chief technician said that the night duty staff were expecting letters of reprimand from me for not being awake at three. I called a meeting of the technical staff to ease their apprehension and create a friendly and open environment. In my three years at the hospital I had no opportunity to reprimand a single staff member.

The AKDN ethical framework states in its opening paragraph:

The Aga Khan Development Network is a contemporary endeavor of the Ismaili Imamat to realize the social conscience of Islam through institutional actions.

About the social conscience of Islam, the Quran says:

Those who spend (freely) whether in prosperity or in adversity; who restrain their anger and pardon men; and Allah loves those who do good. (3: 134)

Imam Jaffar Sadiq said:

"Anger is the key (that opens the door) to all kinds of vices." (Al-Kulayni, al-Kafi, vol. 2, p. 303, Hadith # 3)

Another issue was as disturbing. In my first week in Nairobi, my wife was not well. She had chronic otitis and perhaps the flight had aggravated her condition. I had to see an ENT specialist. A new friend, the head of security and transport at AKUHN and a retired colonel of the Kenya Air Force, introduced me to Dr Din at the doctor's plaza, which is owned by AKUHN.

Dr Din was very professional and did an excellent job. I was still waiting for the medical insurance cards (my entitlement), but Dr Din did not charge me any fee. He gave my wife an antibiotic ear drops prescription and I went to the hospital pharmacy with it. The drops (made in India) were available at 850 Ks, or about $9 US. Unfortunately there was no return change of 150 Ks for my 1000 Ks, and the assistant at the pharmacy informed me that I could get the same medicine across the road (Third Parklands Avenue) in the Medi Plaza complex. I went there and found that the same medicine, with the same batch number, was sold at 250 Ks, but I faced the same problem, there was no change for my 1000 shillings. I slowly walked home. I was staying at the junction of Third Parklands Ave and Kusi Lane. Near my residence was Krishna Plaza, a yellow painted building, and there was a pharmacy there. I tried my luck and the same medicine, same manufacturer, same batch number, similar expiry date, cost only 50 Ks. They gave me 950 Ks in change. I was staggered by the profit margin at AKUHN. Later, after inquiries I came to know that in the hospital pharmacy the profit margin was between 800 to 1000% while in the hospital diagnostic services (laboratory and radiology) it was more than 1500%.

The most expensive hospital in Kenya is AKUHN. It claims on its website to be a nonprofit hospital. Such institutions are funded mostly by charity. In the case of AKUHN, a large percentage of the donors are ordinary Ismailis. Nonprofit hospitals do not pay income or local property taxes, and in return they benefit the community. And so I discovered that in reality maybe AKUHN is not a not-for-profit hospital.

In 2015, I was selected as a mukhi, something like a presiding priest, of the morning session in our Parklands jamatkhana, which is adjacent to AKUHN. At about 5:30 AM one morning, after the prayers, I was called to see an elderly lady who had just fallen down in the darkness at the entrance. I found her left wrist swollen and painful, and I needed to rule out a fracture. My first response was to go to the radiology department for X-rays. She flatly refused to be X-rayed at AKUHN. That same morning at 7:30 AM when I was entering my office I saw her waiting for me outside my office with her X-ray result and a crepe bandage around her wrist. I viewed the result in my office and found that there was only a soft-tissue injury, with no fracture visible. I suggested painkillers and the same crepe bandage to remain. I also told her to see me again if the pain got worse and gave her my mobile number, just in case. She had had her X-ray done at a nearby facility, Jalaram X-ray Unit, at a cost of 2000 Ks. I rang the head of radiology at AKUHN and he informed me that the cost for AP and lateral views would be 12,000 Ks. This was astounding. These few examples clearly indicate that AKUHN is skewed towards providing health care to the very wealthy, in contradiction to the its guiding principles as stated on its website and to the social conscience of Islam.

AKDN institutions serve all without discrimination on the basis of colour, creed, or race. Even the Ismailis, followers of Aga Khan, receive no special favours, though community members have a special attraction in supporting and donating to AKDN institutions. I have talked to many community members informally and the impression is that AKUHN is very expensive even with medical insurance. It is the most expensive hospital in Nairobi. This is not the cry of the few. In October 2018, when the Aga Khan visited Dar es Salaam to commemorate his Diamond Jubilee, in a meeting President Magufuli told him in very clear and simple language that the Aga Khan Hospital in Dar es Salaam was very expensive and it should look into reducing its fees so it could serve more Tanzanians. If anything, the hospital has become more expensive since then.

It is clear that the patients who are treated at AKUHN are mostly the Kenyan elites and foreigners, people who are wealthy. Corruption is high in Kenya, this is not breaking news, and there are many questions as to how wealth is acquired in the country. While I am not suggesting that the hospital should get concerned about how a patient earns their wealth, it should surely assess its impact on the society for which it was created.

I was very disturbed by this issue perhaps because of my own modest background. I therefore went on to investigate the reasons why the AKU hospitals are so expensive.

First, there are too many expatriates employed unnecessarily. Their salary is out of proportion to local standards and they also receive many fringe benefits. One can ask why, after the decades of existence of these hospitals, there is a preference for hiring outsiders over local Kenyans? On average an expatriate pay package would be higher than a local one by a factor of about ten. It's not that the expatriates are better qualified, because locals are also highly qualified and competitive. Unfortunately the attitude persists that expatriates are better performers. There was no document available that specified the salary scale structure. There was academic ranking but salary scales were not defined. It all depended on how one negotiated the starting salary at the time of accepting employment. Even for local employees there was no defined salary structure.

There were positions, especially in the finance department, where expatriates were employed with only undergraduate degrees in business or commerce. In Kenya you can get locals with postgraduate qualifications and corporate experience, but even when they were employed they had to work under the expatriates. Due to the endemic corruption it is still possible to get work permits for expatriates.

It seemed that this problem could easily be resolved. Common sense says why employ a foreigner when an equivalent or even more qualified local is available, and at a much cheaper cost. But I was missing something. The answers to these issues came when the Dean of the Faculty of Medicine selected me to chair the promotion and appointments committee for faculty positions in the Aga Khan Hospitals system for the whole of East Africa. This was when I discovered that the problem was the high level of favouritism in the hiring process. I observed that the staff fell into four recognizable groups. These groups are purely my observation, one would only identify them as groups if one had worked there for some time.

The first group consists of foreigners of European descent, who were mostly from the United States and Canada and were employed mostly in high academic or management positions. They occupy the positions of provost, dean, director, CEO, etc. I guess the aim is to make AKUHN an institution comparable to an American or Canadian university or hospital. For example, the Director of Human Resources was a European based in Karachi! This first group was the highest paid, with unimaginable (to a local person) fringe benefits; some members of this group were airborne most of the time. When I left my position in 2016, even the head of security was a foreigner from the United States. This first group was an exotic, untouchable group.

The second group consisted of Ismailis from the US and Canada. They were originally from East Africa but had emigrated in the 1970s. They did not know Kiswahili (or had forgotten it) and had Canadian and American qualifications. They were highly paid with fringe benefits and had connections with the president of AKU. They seemed aware of major policy decisions and discussions that took place in high-level meetings. One belief of this group was that despite earning the best pay package, which they would never get from their adopted country, they strongly felt that they were doing service for the Imam and for humanity.

The third group was mostly from Pakistan. They were not highly qualified except the few in academia, and would socially gravitate towards each other. They seemed to be there because of the pay and were clearly using the AKUHN as a gateway to enter the west. As chair of the appointments and promotion committee, I had the toughest time dealing with this group, who tended to favour promotions of fellow countrymen and women. In numbers they were the largest expatriate group and occupied sensitive positions (for example in procurement, finance, HR, nursing). I found them offensive and mean. And they did not belong to Kenya.

The last group were the Kenyan Africans (Black) and the Kenyan Ismailis (Asians). The Kenyan Africans were by far the largest group, and a few of them were highly qualified as lecturers and physicians; the rest were nurses, technicians, artisans, clerks, receptionists, drivers, security guards, etc. Their pay was low and they were given hardly any fringe benefits. The turnover of this group was very high; they were the most dissatisfied but had no power or say in any matter. Even those in academic positions were relatively less paid. Kenyan doctors working in the Doctors' Plaza were much better off financially and were powerful as a cohort. The Doctors' Plaza is a four-storey building within the hospital and belongs to the hospital. Private doctors have their clinics here and they pay rent to the hospital and have admitting rights too. Also, academic staff at AKUHN who were clinicians were conducting clinics from the Doctors' Plaza.

The group of Kenyan Ismailis at AKUHN were not highly educated, and very few were in academia. I saw them unfortunately as the silently persecuted group, and I could not understand why. They were few in number and had no voice in the running of the hospital.

In which group did I belong? Due to my country of origin, Tanzania, I got free work permits and unlike foreigners I had to pay taxes and my salary was in local currency, so I was considered a local Ismaili. But because I had a relatively high academic position I floated among all the groups.

During my stay I concluded that the high overhead costs at the hospital and therefore the high cost of services was due to wastage. Not only did the hospital cater mainly to the elite in society, it was administered by an elite. Besides the high salaries of the expatriates, travel was a major expense item. There was a standing joke in the corridors that were AKU to have its own airline it would be profitable. The first group were airborne a lot of the time, travelling in business class. The Swedish ambassador in Tanzania once told me that even ministers in the Swedish cabinet were not privileged to travel business class, tax payers' money only bought cheap economy-class tickets. But at AKU it was different; the higher-ups had the privilege to travel by business class. At one time my nurse boss was working three days in Nairobi and three days in Dar es Salaam.

There are so many anecdotes about AKU travel that I will touch on just a few. In 2014, the CEO and my nurse boss travelled to Indonesia for one night to check on the best available doorknobs, something that could easily be done on the web site of Home Depot or an exclusive hardware site. In 2013, on Saturday, 21 September, there occurred the infamous terrorist attack on West Gate Mall in Nairobi. A few injured victims were brought to AKUHN and I arranged for blood donations. The medical emergency was over within a day. On Friday, September 20, our CEO had departed for Toronto and made a turnaround at Toronto airport to return to Nairobi on Monday, and all this in business class. By Monday life was returning to normal, things were under control in the hospital and she was not a medic, thus, was there a need to spend so much money? When this story was making rounds in the corridor, I heard that she justified her return by saying that she was directed to return by the Chancellor. (The Chancellor of AKU and Chairman of the Board of Trustees is His Highness the Aga Khan.) Whatever the truth, my point is that AKU spends millions on travel. Hopefully with digital platforms easily available and with the experience of coronavirus lockdowns, conferences will not need travel across frontiers.

The annual convocation ceremony takes place on every AKU

campus. In East Africa, it takes place in Nairobi, Dar es Salaam, and Kampala. A big entourage from Karachi visits each of these places, staying at the exclusive Serena hotels. Then there are the ad hoc events, like workshops for staff members held by foreign management experts in expensive hotels. The one such workshop I attended was a total waste of time and resources. None of these workshops are evaluated for impact. Before I joined in 2012 almost all the staff were taken to some national game parks near Nairobi with similar management-efficiency improvement experts.

I saw countless examples of waste and extravagant spending. Frequent travels, expensive hotels, free lunches, the craze for expensive foreign accreditation. I came from a very modest family in a socialist country. I realize that in the business environment in the West, perks are a norm, and my observations may sound like quibbles of a disgruntled employee. My outrage was due to the fact that the practice at AKUHN was exactly the opposite of what I saw in the ethics framework document of its parent, the Aga Khan Development Network. Moreover, when the hospital was built, in its Platinum Jubilee Hospital phase, there were donations made by ordinary Ismaili families of very modest means. The belief was that this was community and public service. Even today, community donations by ordinary folk make up a significant source of the hospital's funding. Wastage and high-flying is hardly an appropriate response to that. There should be accountability.

It is very clear that AKUHN is not a nonprofit organization in the literal sense. It overcharges compared to other institutions and the justification is that it provides the best quality health care. But the costs of care are totally out of proportion to the quality of care provided.

Within the Department of Pathology there were two postgraduate programs, Anatomical Pathology, (includes surgical pathology, cytopathology and forensic pathology) and the other program was Clinical Pathology (includes microbiology, molecular biology, hematology, blood transfusion and chemical pathology). In each of these programs there were on average five students hence at any point in time there were about forty students since the program is of four years duration. Therefore at any time during the working day there will be teaching activities either in the form of case-presentations, journal club, formal lectures, practicals like slide reading and faculty presentations. Apart from this there were also university wide presentations. In all these teaching-learning activities I was actively involved. Outside my department I was also teaching nursing students parasitic infections and took part in the research methodology course that is offered to all first year post graduate students.

Teaching also involved supervising and guiding post graduates with their research and writing their thesis. In the three years I supervised about ten students with their thesis. My research output in three years was six research based published papers in high index journals. I was also involved with the Kenya National Malaria Control under the Ministry of Health.

New leadership and my resignation

Sometime in 2015 we got a new, American CEO at the hospital. His first action was to sack almost 100 Kenyan workers and outsource some of the basic but important services like the laundry. The environment became so toxic, that even my toxic nurse boss could not bear it and left to join the Aga Khan Hospital in Dar-es-Salaam. In this new environment, everything had to be like in the US, and the head of security was imported from there. The new CEO claimed, by his actions, to be an expert in every subject, from surgery and medicine to pathology despite his background of engineering.

In early 2016, the pathologist, Canadian Ismaili decided abruptly to resign due to a misunderstanding with the CEO. This led to delays in reporting the anatomical pathology specimens. While, as chair of the department, I was trying to solve this problem, the CEO decided without any consultation to institute what he referred to as motion study, which would monitor how pathologists spent their time. It was if the remaining anatomical pathologists, who were locals, were lazy. High school kids came from the United States and Canada to the laboratory with stopwatches to monitor even the senior pathologists. The report of the motion study was pathetic. In a basic statistics course it is common knowledge that *"never try to cross a river because it has an average depth of four feet only."* The report gave mean values instead of medians and thus the inferences were flawed and perhaps pre-conceived.

In mid 2016 I realized that it was time to leave, because unilateral decision-making based on intuition without the aid of reason was something I could not be a part of. It was time to leave because what I experienced was that a clean glove was used to hide a dirty hand. I went to the dean and told him that before I tendered my resignation I would give him the basic reason why I was unhappy. I did not want to be part of such a big hypocrisy and falsity that AKUHN was. I do not think he understood me. I left AKUHN exactly three years and twenty-five days after joining.

Research agenda

For any respectable university, research is the cornerstone. There is always hope in life, because there is hope in science. Good research at a university always tries to solve problems in its locality and region. Postgraduate students under the guidance of their supervisors can perform quality research. In any institution students pursuing Masters and PhD degrees have to conduct research for their dissertations, and this research is the best way to obtain scientific evidence and answers that will solve problems. What is needed is a research theme with a number of objectives, and each postgraduate student can select one objective and expand it to a full research proposal. If this is done appropriately, about eighty percent of dissertation research can be published in international or local journals.

I tried to bring about thematic research across AKUHN, but met walls and frontiers within departments. Each student was developing a research question based on the liking of the supervisor and there was lack of coordination. This big pool of students could have easily had an impact on the problems that Kenya is facing in the health field. Let me illustrate this with two examples.

Weak health systems and not singular disease control programs are the major problems in Kenya and much of Sub-Saharan Africa. Whenever there is an outbreak of cholera or any other infectious disease, the impact on morbidity and mortality is relatively high because of the weak health system. The same applies to pandemics like COVID 19. One research theme would be to study the barriers to effective health systems in the region. There can be multiple barriers, such as lack of funds, lack of human resource capacity, poor management of available resources, corruption, poor infrastructure, etc. These could be investigated to provide answers to the problem of poor health systems.

Secondly, Sub-Saharan Africa is facing a double epidemic of infectious and non-communicable diseases. There is no way any country in the region will be able to control NCDs, because of the lack of funds needed to treat them. Think about a person with type II diabetes in a remote village, who requires the drug metformin for the rest of his life. This person has no medical insurance. But through stem cell technology there is hope for a lasting cure, in which case perhaps one day the need for such a drug will not be there. Given the resources and human capacity and possibility of international collaboration, AKU is in the best position to pursue such questions. Unfortunately such targets are not pursued at AKU, and the fragmented approach to postgraduate research aims only to satisfy the qualifying examination requirements.

Because of nepotism, group gravitation, and unfair remuneration, the local faculty is hardly interested in developing the academic culture of effective research. This is a big and a complex challenge that AKU is facing at its Nairobi campus.

12

Life in Nairobi

I had initially thought that relocating from Dar es Salaam to Nairobi would be difficult and we would have to make a lot of adjustments, but this was not the case and in a short time we were enjoying Nairobi life outside AKU. Zeenat, especially, liked Nairobi and even today she would prefer to retire in Nairobi rather than Dar es Salaam. It was possible for Zeenat to seek employment, but she decided to retire and be a full-time housekeeper.

Two things about Nairobi made our settling down easier. First, the Kiswahili spoken by Kenyans is very different. They cannot finish a sentence in Kiswahili without using an English word. Their pronunciation is also different. We spoke the coastal version of Kiswahili fluently, while it was uncommon for Nairobi Asians to speak or communicate in it; many did not even understand simple words. So when Zeenat and I spoke Kiswahili it fascinated the local population. There is a food market opposite the Aga Khan Hospital where many people shop. Zeenat was well known there and many women with food stalls called her Mama Swahili. In a short time I was invited to Nairobi University to be its external examiner for medical students. One day, driving back from the University, somewhere near the Silver Springs roundabout I missed the correct exit and went the wrong way. I realized immediately that I was going the wrong way, so I did a U-turn and the traffic cop at the round-about stopped me. I spoke Kiswahili with him, explaining my plight, that I had intended to go to the Aga Khan Hospital at Limuru and Third Parklands. He called all the six traffic policemen who were there to hear my explanation in Kiswahili. It ended well as one of them volunteered to accompany me till Limuru Road.

The second thing about Nairobi is that the women are very entrepreneurial. For example, women vendors go from house to house selling vegetables and fruits; if an item is missing, they immediately phone their team member to bring it. Zeenat was very popular with them and they made their meeting place outside our house. They would sit on our veranda counting takes and Zeenat would give them water to drink and stop to chat with them. This made her conspicuous—an Asian woman in Nairobi having such close and friendly relations with the women vendors. But she was having a good time and also getting the best vegetables and fruits at a cheaper price.

In Nairobi there is a neighbourhood known as Eastleigh, east of the central business district; it is also known as Small Mogadishu because almost all the shops belong to the people from Somalia. It is famous for its shops; almost anything is available there and at a much lower cost. On Saturdays we would take the popular public buses known as matatus (in Kiswahili *matatu* means "three," these buses were never considered full, they always had room for three more passengers) to Eastleigh and shop there for non-perishable items. The cost was about fifty percent less. Asian women, friends of Zeenat, found it incredible that we went shopping in Eastleigh, because there was an inherent fear in them that it was not safe to go there. But we found it very safe, and people were very respectful and friendly.

We made many friends in Nairobi, both Africans and within the Ismaili community. Opposite our house on Kusi Lane, there were the jua kali ("hot sun") stalls selling freshly cooked food at cheap prices. The women vendors we knew would buy their lunch there before coming to relax on our veranda. The jua kali guys would take water from our tap and were also very friendly. All this was important because security and safety in Nairobi is a big issue. Having good neighbours and being surrounded by friendly people gave us a sense of comfort and protection. It was rare that we went out at night, because after six PM Nairobi streets become deserted, and there are only vehicles about. Security in Nairobi is indeed a major issue.

13

Real Retirement in Calgary

I am facing an uncertain future with humour, grace, and dignity but perhaps there is an antidote to uncertainty . . .

No one has ever asked me to my face who I really am. My contention is that I am a Tanzanian by birth and a Tanzanian by choice. My relocation to Calgary in Canada is based purely on my social circumstances and with time hopefully I will return to Tanzania. The Kiswahili adage, *Angepaa kipingu, marejeo ni mtini*—the eagle may soar upwards but he will return to his tree— applies here to me.

I am writing this last chapter of my story in the midst of the Covid-19 pandemic. The pandemic has drastically changed our lives; these unprecedented changes are having a toll on everybody. Almost eighty percent of the world is somehow in a lockdown mode and the future remains uncertain. The health systems of even the richest countries are overwhelmed and near collapsing. Apart from the human health impact in terms of morbidity and mortality, it is the economic impact that is most worrisome. What the final cost of coronavirus will be is sheer guesswork. The most fearful and panic-causing issue is that so little is known about the virus. It will take time for science and medicine to discover more.

After my three-year stay with the AKUHN in Nairobi I decided to relocate to Calgary in Canada. The main reason for moving to Canada was to help take care of my grandchildren and also enable my daughter-in-law to restart her career after almost seven years of staying at home.

I arrived in Calgary on August 26, 2016 to start my retirement. As I write this, it's almost three years and a few months that I have been in Calgary. Am I missing Nairobi? For sure I do not miss AKUHN, but I do miss my teaching and research activities. Do I miss Dar es Salaam, yes I miss the environment of Dar es Salaam, where I worked for almost forty years. I have close friends there, people I have known for most of my life; I know the city well; its politics, its social dynamics, all this I miss; but if I were to move to Dar es Salaam, I think I would miss my grandchildren more than anything else. So this is indeed a dilemma and once my grandkids become teenagers, I will have to give them their space but still somehow remain connected and enjoy being a grandfather of teenagers.

During the first year I took time to walk around and get used to the area where I stay. Now I am well acquainted with the Varsity area in North West Calgary. This place according to me is the best place in the world. It is very safe; there are a lot of open spaces and lots of safe walking paths. Public places like the Calgary Library at Crowfoot are a wonderful place to spend time; nearby there is a well-equipped YMCA gym. I have invested in my health by taking long walks when the weather allows and going to the gym. Today I am in better shape than I was in Nairobi and life is much less stressful.

Calgary is very different from either Nairobi or Dar es Salaam, which are crowded, noisy, polluted, and in some places unsafe. The other main difference is the systemic strength of social institutions.

The Alberta Health Service is very client-friendly and at the age we are, Zeenat and I need regular medical check-ups. In the past four years or so in Calgary I have never been stopped by a policeman for any reason; in Kenya or Tanzania, a week would not pass by without having some sort of encounter with the police. Initially this seemed odd but now I am used to the fact that a law-abiding citizen in Calgary may not have an encounter with the police for years. From my short stay here in Calgary, it seems this place is like heaven on earth but just wait for late fall or winter to start.

All the four winters I have experienced have been severely cold and to be outdoors for more than ten minutes is impossible for me. We both miss the weather of Nairobi and Dar es Salaam then. This weather disadvantage is not in anyone's control, I hear even those who are born in Calgary never get used to the severe winters. Apart from severe winters, the rest of the seasons like spring and summer are very comfortable and enjoyable. The summer of 2020 was exceptionally warm and we took advantage of that to visit a number of tourist sites near Calgary.

Notwithstanding all these advantages and comforts in Calgary, I would still prefer hot and humid Dar es Salaam, but there is a dilemma. My life partner Zeenat is quite adamant that there is no moving back to East Africa. In due course we will need to solve this issue amicably, perhaps spend Calgary winters in Dar es Salaam and return in early spring to Calgary.

Sometime in 2018, my son introduced me to the concept of strength training, and I also did a lot of reading around the subject, learned the techniques and correct forms for lifting weights to avoid injury and today both myself and my wife do strength training every single day. This has had an immense impact on my health. My blood sugar and blood pressure are well in control and overall I feel much better physically and mentally.

One day while I was walking on the track at the gym, I met a lady aged eighty-nine who insisted that while walking I should carry dumbbells of at least ten pounds in each hand. She explained that this is known as a farmer's walk. She was a retired urologist and was in remission for cancer of the larynx and at her age she was doing the farmer's walk with twenty-five pounds in each hand. This was a most enlightening episode and today I do the walk with thirty pounds in each hand. I am now totally convinced that notwithstanding one's age strength training or resistance training as some call it is the best way to remain healthy and avoid frailty. In addition, one should also perform cardio exercises such as long walks, stairs climbing, or HIIT training (high intensity interval training).

I am witnessing a big paradox that perhaps has been created intentionally by the Big Pharma and related industries. There is a belief among many people in North America (and worldwide) that there is a pill for everything. Of course medicines are useful, both natural and pharmaceutical. But the notion that your lifestyle can make you vulnerable to illness and therefore you should change your lifestyle to get healthy has not taken hold.

In Calgary I also started writing for Tanzania's daily newspaper *The Citizen*. This hobby of writing once a week has kept me busy. I also keep up with what is happening back home. I have written more than sixty articles for the paper and have received very positive feedback. I have written on a wide range of topics, from politics to health and education and given an honest opinion on whatever was current. In December 2019 I stopped writing my articles, in order to finish this book.

What is happiness?

Happiness, actually, is an illusion, it is a saleable item in our world. Religions, governments, and self-styled experts constantly put up this illusory, marketable commodity for sale. Everybody seems to be chasing happiness around us. In simple terms, happiness is a range of positive emotions, including joy, pride, contentment, and gratitude, a feeling of subjective well being. How many of us attain it? Today, reflecting on the life I have lived and what really brought me happiness, the first thing that comes to mind is that I have been able to put food on the table for my family. I come from a humble background in a poor family in a modest country. During my childhood in Morogoro and Tanga there were days when we had only one meal per day; that feeling, that experience lingers in my mind, and the thought that my life has changed for the better, and for the betterment of my family, gives me a lot of happiness.

Two qualities that I value most are simplicity and humility. When my son was born, that was one of the happiest moments in my life, and now when I see that bright shining glow in the eyes of my grandkids I feel as happy. My grandkids frequently remind me how old I am and repeat to me my age; they do not know that I need no telling, because my bladder constantly sends me reminders. Ageing is not in our control. There is a lot that is being said about ageing gracefully and with dignity; but no one I have met wants to age. One just accepts it. If you feel that you are entitled to be comfortable and happy at all times, that everything is supposed to be just exactly the way you want it, you are cultivating unhappiness. It is a sickness and it will eat into your life. You will see every adversity as injustice, every challenge as a failure, every inconvenience as a personal slight, every disagreement as a betrayal. You will be confined to your own petty skull-sized hell, burning with entitlement, and bluster running in circles around you. What I have concluded in my life is that to grow old is to pass from passion to compassion. But in all honesty I miss my youthful life all the time, but the truth of life is that you can't unscramble age.

Aging has instilled in me a sense of satisfaction, which perhaps was in short supply when I was young and active. Plato has been ascribed to say, "Poverty consists, not in the decrease of one's possessions, but in the increase of one's greed," but what I saw in my lifetime among the rural, poor population in Tanzania was more satisfaction and gratitude. Success can be a goal without a satiation point. I am reminded of the donkey driver who kept his beast moving by dangling a carrot attached to a stick. With all the technological advancement we have, do we really want to be like the donkey, running all the time for the unreachable carrot?

I have made much effort to communicate my story. I think of it as a work of translation, one that tries to build a bridge towards readers. The study of human medicine, especially public health, can be technical as well as human. I hope I have learned from both.

Epilogue

In the following appendices are a list of my academic achievements over forty years. During that time I learnt that "No matter how large the calf, it must kneel to suck at its mother's breast" (Igbo proverb). There is no tangible achievement without teamwork. All that I achieved during my lifetime is because of teamwork. In medicine any one patient gets better because of contributions from all the members of the clinical team, similarly in public health when all the diverse fields converge there is a positive outcome.

My family, Morogoro, 1962. From left to right: Aziz, Mom, Dad, Gulshan, myself. Back row, L to R: Shamshun and Nizar. Missing is my eldest sister Zehrakhanu.

1965. Class six at Aga Khan Primary School in Tanga. Listening to educational broadcast.

1966. Receiving the Best Boy trophy from Regional Education Officer of Tanga.

1969. Parade at Chidya Secondary School. I was in form IV.

1974. At Muhimbili after the final examination of Certificate in Medical Laboratory Technology. I look worried because I was the only student who had a negative result in the pregnancy test. The rest had a positive result. Turned out it was urine from a male thus I was correct.

1976. My wedding to my life partner to date, Zeenat.

1985. Graduation, University of Dar es Salaam; the only sibling in my family to go to university and qualify as Medical Doctor. All credit goes to my wife Zeenat for her untiring support and sacrifice. Hers is a key role played in silence.

1996. PhD defense at Karolinska Institutet, in Stockholm.

Appendix 1

Professional Qualifications

Academic

PhD (Infectious Diseases) Karolinska, Sweden. (1996) Thesis: Malaria control measures: Impact on malaria and anaemia in a holoendemic area of rural coastal Tanzania
MSc (Medical Parasitology) London School of Hygiene & Tropical Medicine. (1989)
Diploma in Tropical Medicine & Hygiene (DTM & H) London. (1989)
Doctor of Medicine (MD) University of Dar es Salaam. (1985)
Diploma in Medical Laboratory Technology (DMLT) University of Dar es Salaam. (1977)
Certificate in Medical Laboratory Technology (CMLT) University of Dar es Salaam. (1974)

Career Summary

1. Chair & Professor, Department of Pathology, Aga Khan University Hospital Nairobi, Kenya. July-2013 to August 2016
2. Professor, Department of Parasitology/Medical. Entomology, School of Public Health & Social Sciences, Muhimbili University of Health & Allied Sciences, (MUHAS) Dar es Salaam, Tanzania.
3. Director Postgraduate Studies: MUHAS from 2009 to 2012.
4. Associate Professor, Department of Parasitology/Medical. Entomology School of Public Health & Social Sciences, Muhimbili University of Health & Allied Sciences, Dar es Salaam, Tanzania. 2001
5. Senior Lecturer & Head, Department of Parasitology/Medical. Entomology Institute of Public Health, Muhimbili University College of Health Sciences, Dar es Salaam, Tanzania. 1997–2001
6. Lecturer, Department of Parasitology/Medical. Entomology 1992–1997
7. Assistant Lecturer, Department of Parasitology/Medical. Entomology 1989–1992
8. Tutorial Assistant, Department of Parasitology/Medical. Entomology 1986–1988
9. Chief Medical Laboratory Technician, Department of Pediatrics, Faculty of Medicine.1977–1980

Memberships and Appointments

East African Society for Parasitologists
American Society of Tropical Medicine & Hygiene
Advisory Committee, National Malaria Control, Tanzania
Board, Institute of Public Health
Board, Faculty of Medicine (1997-2002)
WHO Expert Task Force on Insecticide Impregnated Bed Nets. (1996-1999)
WHO Task Force—Multilateral Initiative for Malaria MIM (2001-2006)

WHO Task Force on Malaria Research Capability Strengthening in Africa, (MIM) (2001-2006)

Editorial Board—ACTA TROPICA

Editorial Board, *The Dar Graduate: Journal of the University of Dar es Salaam Convocation*

Data safety monitoring board of two clinical trials under WHO and NIH

MMV-Medicines for Malaria Ventures—global initiative based in Geneva. ESAC member (2004-2008)

DSMB of malaria vaccine trials in Africa and Consortium for malaria in pregnancy

Course Coordinator, Masters in Public Health. A joint collaborative project of Institute of Public Health, Tanzania & Heidelberg University, Germany

Chairperson Elect, Tanzania Public Health Association (2000-2004)

Appendix 2

Professional Publications

Abdulla, Salim, Issaka Sagara, Steffen Borrmann, Umberto D'Alessandro, Raquel González, Mary Hamel, Bernhards Ogutu, Andreas Mårtensson, John Lyimo, Hamma Maiga, Philip Sasi, Alain Nahum, Quique Bassat, Elizabeth Juma, Lucas Otieno, Anders Björkman, Hans Peter Beck, Kim Andriano, Marc Cousin, Gilbert Lefèvre, David Ubben, & Zulfikarali Premji. "Efficacy and safety of artemether-lumefantrine dispersible tablets compared with crushed commercial tablets in African infants and children with uncomplicated malaria: a randomised, single-blind, multicentre trial." *The Lancet*, Volume 372, Issue 9652, Pages 1819–1827, 22 November 2008.

Ahmad, Rushdy, Liangxia Xie, Margaret Pyle, Marta F. Suarez, Tobias Broger, Dan Steinberg, Shaali M Ame, Marilla G Lucero, Matthew J Szucs, Melanie MacMullan, Frode S Berven, Arup Dutta, Diozele M Sanvictores, Veronica L Tallo, Robert Bencher, Dominic P Eisinger, Usha Dhingra, Saikat Deb, Said M Ali, Saurabh Mehta, Wafaie W Fawzi, Ian D Riley, Sunil Sazawal, Zul Premji, Robert Black, Christopher JL Murray, Bill Rodriguez, Steven A Carr, David R Walt, & Michael A Gillette. "A rapid triage test for active pulmonary tuberculosis in adult patients with persistent cough." *Sci. Transl. Med.* 11, eaaw8287.

Alin, MH, CM Kihamia, A Bjorkman, BA Bwijo, Z Premji, GJ Mtey, & M Ashton. "Efficacy of oral and intravenous artesunate in male Tanzanian adults with *Plasmodium falciparum* malaria and in vitro susceptibility to artemisinin, chloroquine, and mefloquine." *The American Journal of Tropical Medicine and Hygiene*, 53, 639-45.

Alloueche, A, W Bailey, S Barton, J Bwika, P Chimpeni, CO Falade, FA Fehintola, J Horton, S Jaffar, T Kanyok, PG, Kremsner, JG Kublin, T Lang, MA Missinou, C Mkandala, AMJ Oduola, Z Premji, L Robertson, A Sowunmi, SA Ward, & PA Winstanley. "Comparison of chlorproguanil-dapsone with sulfadoxine-pyrimethaminefor the treatment of uncomplicated falciparum malaria in young African children: double-randomised controlled trial." *Lancet* 2004; 363: 1843-48.

Aponte, John J, David Schellenberg, Andrea Egan, Alasdair Breckenridge, Ilona Carneiro, Julia Critchley, Ina Danquah, Alexander Dodoo, Robin Kobbe, Bertrand Lell, Jürgen May, Zul Premji, Sergi Sanz, Esperanza Sevene, Rachida Soulaymani-Becheikh, Peter Winstanley, Samuel Adjei, Sylvester Anemana, Daniel Chandramohan, Saadou Issifou, Frank Mockenhaupt, Seth Owusu-Agyei, Brian Greenwood, Martin P Grobusch, Peter G Kremsner, Eusebio Macete, Hassan Mshinda, Robert D Newman, Laurence Slutsker, Marcel Tanner, Pedro Alonso, & Clara Menendez. "Efficacy and safety of intermittent preventive treatment with sulfadoxine-pyrimethamine for malaria in African infants: a pooled analysis of six randomised, placebo-controlled trials." *The Lancet*, Volume 374, Issue 9700, Pages 1533–1542, 31 October.

Aydin-Schmidt, Berit, Marycelina Mubi, Ulrika Morris, Max Petzold, Billy E Ngasala,

Zul Premji, Anders Björkman, & Andreas Mårtensson. "Usefulness of *Plasmodium falciparum*-specific rapid diagnostic tests for assessment of parasite clearance and detection of recurrent infections after artemisinin-based combination therapy." *Malaria Journal* 2013, 12:349, http://www.malariajournal.com/content/12/1/349.

Bates, Sarah J, Peter A Winstanley, William M Watkins, Ali Alloueche, Juma Bwika, T Christian Happi, Peter G. Kremsner, James G Kublinm, Zul Premji, & Carol Hopkins Sibley. "Rare, highly pyrimethamine-resistant alleles of *Plasmodium falciparum* dihydrofolate reductase from five African sites." *The Journal of Infectious Diseases* 2004:190 (15 November).

Bei, Amy K, Christopher D Membi, Julian C Rayner, Marycelina Mubi, Billy Ngasala, Ali A Sultan, Zul Premji, & Manoj T Duraisingh. "Variant merozoite protein expression is associated with erythrocyte invasion phenotypes in *Plasmodium falciparum* isolates from Tanzania." *Molecular and biochemical parasitology* 2007;153 (1):66-71.

Beutler, Ernest, Stephan Duparc, & the G6PD Deficiency Working Group. "Glucose-6-Phosphate Dehydrogenase Deficiency and Antimalarial Drug Development." *The American Journal of Tropical Medicine and Hygiene*, 77(4), 2007, pp. 779-789.

Brabin BJ, Z Premji, & F Verhoeff. "An analysis of anaemia and childhood mortality." *The Journal of Nutrition*, Feb 131 (2S-2): 636S-645S.

Carlsson, Anja M, Billy E Ngasala, Sabina Dahlström, Christopher Membi, Isabel M Veiga, Lars Rombo, Salim Abdulla, Zul Premji, J Pedro Gil, Anders Björkman, & Andreas Mårtensson. "*Plasmodium falciparum* population dynamics during the early phase of anti-malarial drug treatment in Tanzanian children with acute uncomplicated malaria." *Malar J* 2011, 10(1):380.

Duggan, Christopher, William MacLeod, Nancy F Krebs, Jamie L Westcott, Wafaie W Fawzi, Zul G Premji, Victor Mwanakasale, Jonathon L Simon, Kojo Yeboah-Antwi, Davidson H Hamer, & the Zinc Against Plasmodium Study Group. "Plasma Zinc Concentrations Are Depressed during the Acute Phase Response in Children with Falciparum Malaria." *The Journal of Nutrition*, 135: 802-807.

Ekvall, H, P Arese, F Turrini, K Ayi, F Mannu, Z Premji, & A Bjorkman. "Acute haemolysis in childhood falciparum malaria." *Transactions of The Royal Society of Tropical Medicine and Hygiene*, 95, 611-617.

Ekvall H, Z Premji, & A Björkman. "Micronutrient and iron supplementation and effective anti-malarial treatment synergistically improve childhood anaemia." *Tropical Medicine & International Health*, 5, 696-705.

Ekvall, H, Z Premji, & A Björkman. "Chloroquine treatment for uncomplicated childhood malaria aggravates anaemia in a drug resistant area of Tanzania." *Transactions of the Royal Society of Tropical Medicine and Hygiene*, 92, 556-560.

Ekvall H, Z Premji, S Bennett, & A Björkman. "Haemoglobin concentration in children in a malaria holoendemic area is determined by cumulated *Plasmodium falciparum* parasite densities." *The American Journal of Tropical Medicine and Hygiene*, 64, 58-66.

Eshel, Yochay, Arnon Houri-Yafin, Hagai Benkuzari, Natalie Lezmy, Mamta Soni, Malini Charles, Jayanthi Swaminathan, Hilda Solomon, Pavithra Sampathkumar,

Zul Premji, Caroline Mbithi, Zaitun Nneka, Simon Onsongo, Daniel Maina, Sarah Levy-Schreier, Caitlin Lee Cohen, Dan Gluck, Joseph Joel Pollak, & Seth J Salpeter. "Evaluation of the Parasight Platform for Malaria Diagnosis." March 2017 Volume 55 Issue 3 *Journal of Clinical Microbiology* jcm.asm.org 768.

Falade, Catherine, Michael Makanga, Zul Premji, Christine-Elke Ortmann, Marlies Stockmeyer, & Patricia Ibarra de Palacios. "Efficacy and safety of artemether—lumefantrine (Coartem®) tablets (six-dose regimen) in African infants and children with acute, uncomplicated falciparum malaria." *Transactions of the Royal Society of Tropical Medicine & Hygiene*, 99, 459-467.

Fataki M, M Karim, & Z Premji. "Rising trend of malaria morbidity and mortality in children at Muhimbili National Hospital." TMJ vol 17, no 2.

Gasarasi, DB, Z Premji, PGM Mujinja, & C Makwaya. "Gender differences in the clinical manifestations of lymphatic filariasis in Rufiji District, South East Tanzania." *Tanzania Medical Journal*, Vol 17, No 1,4-9.

Gasarasi, DB, Z Premji, PGM Mujinja, & R Mpembeni. "Acute Adenolymphangitis due to Bancroftian filariasis in Rufiji District, South East Tanzania." *Acta Tropica*, 75, 19-28.

Hamer, DH, WB MacLeod, E Addo-Yobo, CP Duggan, B Estrella, WW Fawzi, JK Konde-Lule, V Mwanakasale, ZG Premji, F Sempértegui, FP Ssengooba, K Yeboah-Antwi, & JL Simon. "Age, temperature, and parasitaemia predict chloroquine treatment failure and anaemia in children with uncomplicated *Plasmodium falciparum* malaria." *Transactions of the Royal Society of Tropical Medicine and Hygiene.* Jul-Aug;97 (4):422-8.

Hellgren, U, CM Kihamia, Y Bergqvist, M Lebbad, Z Premji, & L Rombo. "Standard and reduced doses of sulfadoxine-pyrimethamine for treatment of *Plasmodium falciparum* in Tanzania, with determination of drug concentrations and susceptibility in vitro." *Transactions of the Royal Society of Tropical Medicine and Hygiene*, 84, 469-72.

Hellgren, U, CM Kihamia, Z Premji, & K Danielson. "Local anaesthetic cream for the alleviation of pain during venepuncture in Tanzanian schoolchildren." *The British Journal of Clinical Pharmacology*, 28 205-6.

Hietala, Sofia Friberg, Andreas Mårtensson, Billy Ngasala, Sabina Dahlström, Niklas Lindegårdh, Anna Annerberg, Zul Premji, Anna Färnert, Pedro Gil, Anders Björkman, & Michael Ashton. "Population Pharmacokinetics and pharmacodynamics of artemether and lumefantrine during combination treatment in children with uncomplicated falciparum malaria in Tanzania." *Antimicrobial Agents and Chemothery,* 2010, 54:4780–4788.

Hirji, Karim F, & Zulfiqarali G Premji. "Pre-referral rectal artesunate in severe malaria: a flawed trial." *Trials* 2011, 12:188 doi:10.1186/1745-6215-12-188.

Hugosson, E, SM Montgomery, Z Premji, M Troye-Blomberg, & A Björkman. "Higher IL – 10 levels are associated with less effective clearance of *Plasmodium falciparum* parasites." *Parasite immunology* 26. 111-117.

Hugosson, Elisabeth, Donath Tarimo, Marita Troye-Blomberg, Scott M. Montgomery, Zul Premji, & Anders Björkman. "Antipyretic, parasitologic, and immunologic effects of combining sulfadoxine/pyrimethamine with chloroquine or paracetamol for treating uncomplicated *plasmodium falciparum* malaria." *The American Journal of Tropical Medicine and Hygiene*, 69 (4), pp. 366-371.

Hugosson, Elisabeth, Scott M Montgomery, Zul Premji, Marita Troye-Blomberg, & Anders Björkman. "Relationship between antipyretic effects and cytokine levels in uncomplicated falciparum malaria during different treatment regimes." *Acta Tropica*, 99 (1): 75-82.

Hyder, Adnan A, Suzanne Maman, Joyce E Nyoni, Shaniysa A Khasiani, Noreen Teoh, Zul Premji, & Salim Sohani. "The pervasive triad of food security, gender inequity and women's health: exploratory research from sub-Saharan Africa." *African Health Sciences*, Vol 5 No 4.

Joseph, Deokary, Abdunoor M Kabanywanyi, Ruth Hulser, Zulfiqarali Premji, Omary MS Minzi, & Kefas Mugittu. "Exploration of in vivo efficacy of artemether lumefantrine against uncomplicated *Plasmodium falciparum* malaria in under-fives in Tabora region, Tanzania." *Malaria Journal* 2013, 12:60 http://www.malariajournal.com/content/12/1/60.

Kassim, Ali, Valentin Pflüger, Zul Premji, Claudia Daubenbergerand, & Gunturu Revathi. "Comparison of biomarker based Matrix Assisted Laser Desorption Ionization-Time of Flight Mass Spectrometry (MALDI-TOF MS) and conventional methods in the identification of clinically relevant bacteria and yeast." BMC Microbiology (2017) 17:128 DOI 10.1186/s12866-017-1037-z.

Keiser, J, J Utzinger, Z Premji, Y Yamagata, & BH Singer. "Acridine-Orange for malaria diagnosis: its promotion and implementation in Tanzania, and the implications for malaria control." *Annals of Tropical Medicine & Parasitology*, vol 96, No 7, 643-654.

Kern, Steven E, Alfred B Tiono, Michael Makanga, Adama Dodji Gbado, Zulfiqarali Premji, Oumar Gaye, Issaka Sagara, David Ubben, Marc Cousin, Fiyinfolu Oladiran, Oliver Sander, & Bernhards Ogutu. "Community screening and treatment of asymptomatic carriers of *Plasmodium falciparum* with artemether-lumefantrine to reduce malaria disease burden: a modeling and simulation analysis." *Malaria Journal* 2011, 10:210 doi:10.1186/1475-2875-10-21.

Kidima, Winifrida B, Gamba Nkwengulila, Zul Premji, Allen L Malisa, & H Mshinda. "Dhfr and dhps mutations in *Plasmodium falciparum* isolates in Mlandizi, Kibaha, Tanzania: association clinical outcome." *Tanzania Health Research Bulletin* Vol. 8 No. 2 May 2006.

Mahende, Coline, Billy Ngasala, John Lusingu, Allvan Butichi, Paminus Lushino, Martha Lemnge, & Zul Premji. "Aetiology of acute febrile episodes in children attending Korogwe District Hospital in North-Eastern Tanzania." *PLoS One*. 2014 Aug 4;9(8):e104197. doi: 10.1371/journal.pone.0104197. eCollection 2014.

Mahende, Coline, Billy Ngasala, John Lusingu, Allvan Butichi, Paminus Lushino, Martha Lemnge, Bruno Mmbando, & Zul Premji. "Bloodstream bacterial infection among outpatient children with acute febrile illness in North-Eastern Tanzania." *BMC Research Notes* 2015, 8:289. doi:10.1186/s13104-015-1178-9.

Mahende, Coline, Billy Ngasala, John Lusingu, Tai-Soon Yong, Paminus Lushino, Martha Lemnge, Bruno Mmbando, & Zul Premji. "Performance of rapid diagnostic test, blood-film microscopy and PCR for the diagnosis of malaria infection among febrile children from Korogwe District, Tanzania." *Malaria Journal* 2016, 15:391 (26 July 2016). doi: 10.1186/s12936-016-1450-z.

Mahende, Coline, Billy Ngasala, John Lusingu, Thomas Mårtensson, Paminus Lushino, Martha Lemnge, Bruno Mmbando, & Zul Premji. "Profile of C-reactive protein, white cells and neutrophil populations in febrile children from rural north-eastern Tanzania." (Submitted).

Makanga, Michael, Quique Bassat, Catherine O Falade, Zulfiqarali G Premji, Srivicha Krudsood, Philip Hunt, Verena Walter, Hans-Peter Beck, Anne-Claire Marrast, Marc Cousin, & Philip J Rosenthal. "Efficacy and Safety of Artemether-Lumefantrine in the Treatment of Acute, Uncomplicated *Plasmodium falciparum* Malaria: A Pooled Analysis." *Am. J. Trop. Med. Hyg.*, 85(5), 2011, pp. 793–804 doi:10.4269/ajtmh.2011.11-0069.

Makanga, Michael, Zul Premji, Catherine Falade, Juntra Karbwang, Edgar A Mueller, Kim Andriano, Philip Hunt, & Patricia Ibarra de Palacios. "Efficacy and safety of six-dose regimen of artemether—lumefantrine (Coartem®) tablets in paediatrics with uncomplicated *Plasmodium falciparum* malaria: A pooled analysis of individual data." *The American Journal of Tropical Medicine and Hygiene*, 74 (6), pp. 991-998.

Makemba, AM, P Winch, VM Makame, GL Mehl, Z Premji, JN Minjas, CJ Shiff. "Treatment practices for degedege, a locally recognized febrile illness, and implications for strategies to decrease mortality from severe malaria in Bagamoyo District, Tanzania." *Tropical Medicine & International Health*, 1, 305-13.

Malmberg, Maja, Billy Ngasala, Pedro E Ferreira, Erik Larsson, Irina Jovel, Angelica Hjalmarsson, Max Petzold, Zul Premji, José P Gil, Anders Björkman, & Andreas Mårtensson. "Temporal trends of molecular markers associated with artemether-lumefantrine tolerance/resistance in Bagamoyo district, Tanzania." *Malaria Journal* 2013, 12:103 http://www.malariajournal.com/content/12/1/103.

Mårtensson, Andreas, Billy Ngasala, Johan Ursing, M Isabel Veiga, Lisa Wiklund, Christopher Membi, Scott M Montgomery, Zul Premji, Anna Färnert, & Anders Björkman. "Influence of consecutive-day blood sampling on polymerase chain reaction-adjusted parasitological cure rates in an antimalarial-drug trial conducted in Tanzania." *The Journal of Infectious Diseases*, 2007;195 (4):597-601.

Mfaume, SM, P Winch, AM Makemba, & Z Premji. "Mosques against malaria." World Health Forum 18: 1 35-38.

Mubi, Marycelina, Annika Janson, Marian Warsame, Andreas Mårtensson, Karin Källander, Max G Petzold, Billy Ngasala, Gloria Maganga, Lars L Gustafsson, Amos Massele, Göran Tomson, Zul Premji, & Anders Björkman. "Malaria Rapid Testing by Community Health Workers Is Effective and Safe for Targeting Malaria Treatment: Randomised Cross-Over Trial in Tanzania." *PLoS One.* 2011; 6(7): e19753. Published online 2011 July 5. doi: 10.1371/journal.pone.0019753.

Mubi, Marycelina, Deodatus Kakoko, Billy Ngasala, Zul Premji, Stefan Peterson, Anders Björkman, & Andreas Mårtensson. "Malaria diagnosis and treatment practices following introduction of rapid diagnostic tests in Kibaha District, Coast Region, Tanzania." *Malaria Journal* 2013, 12:293, http://www.malariajournal.com/content/12/1/293.

Mugittu, Kefas, Modesta Ndejembi, Allen Malisa, Martha Lemnge, Zulfikar Premji, Alex Mwita, Watoky Nyka, Johannes Kataraihya, Salim Abdullah, Hans-Peter Beck, & Hassan Mshinda. "Therapeutic efficacy of Sulfadoxine-Pyrimethamine and prevalence of resistance markers in Tanzania: prior to revision of malaria treatment policy. *Plasmodium falciparum*, dihydrofolate reductase and dihydropteroate synthase mutations in monitoring in vivo resistance." *The American Journal of Tropical Medicine and Hygiene*, 71 (6), pp. 696-702.

Murray, Christopher JL, Alan D Lopez, Robert Black, Ramesh Ahuja, Said Mohd Ali, Abdullah Baqui, Lalit Dandona, Emily Dantzer, Vinita Das, Usha Dhingra, Arup Dutta, Wafaie Fawzi, Abraham D Flaxman, Sara Gomez, Bernardo Hernandez, Rohina Joshi, Henry Kalter, Aarti Kumar, Vishwajeet Kumar, Rafael Lozano, Marilla Lucero, Saurabh Mehta, Bruce Neal, Summer Lockett Ohno, Rajendra Prasad, Devarsetty Praveen, Zul Premji, Dolores Ramirez-Villalobos, Hazel Remolador, Ian Riley, Minerva Romero, Mwanaidi Said, Diozele Sanvictores, Sunil Sazawaland, & Veronica Tallo. "Population Health Metrics Research Consortium gold standard verbal autopsy validation study: design, implementation, and development of analysis datasets." *Population Health Metrics* 2011, 9:27 doi:10.1186/1478-7954-9-27 Published: 4 August 2011.

Murray, Christopher JL, Rafael Lozano, Abraham D Flaxman, Peter Serina, David Phillips, Andrea Stewart, Spencer L James, Alireza Vahdatpour, Charles Atkinson, Michael K Freeman, Summer Lockett Ohno, Robert Black, Said Mohammed Ali, Abdullah H Baqui, Lalit Dandona, Emily Dantzer, Gary L Darmstadt, Vinita Das, Usha Dhingra, Arup Dutta, Wafaie Fawzi, Sara Gómez, Bernardo Hernández, Rohina Joshi, Henry D Kalter, Aarti Kumar, Vishwajeet Kumar, Marilla Lucero, Saurabh Mehta, Bruce Neal, Devarsetty Praveen, Zul Premji, Dolores Ramírez-Villalobos, Hazel Remolador, Ian Riley, Minerva Romero, Mwanaidi Said, Diozele Sanvictores, Sunil Sazawal, Veronica Tallo, & Alan D Lopez. "Using verbal autopsy to measure causes of death: the comparative performance of existing methods." *BMC Medicine* 2014, 12:5 doi:10.1186/1741-7015-12-5 Published: 9 January 2014.

Mwaiswelo, Richard, Billy Ngasala, Irina Jovel, Berit Aydin-Schmidt, Roland Gosling, Zul Premji, Bruno Mmbando, Anders Björkman, & Andreas Mårtensson. "Adding a single low-dose of primaquine (0.25 mg/kg) to artemether-lumefantrine did not compromise treatment outcome of uncomplicated *Plasmodium falciparum* malaria in Tanzania: a randomized, single-blinded clinical trial." Malar J. 2016; 15: 435.

Mwaiswelo, Richard, Billy Ngasala, Irina Jovel, Roland Gosling, Zul Premji, Eugenie Poirot, Bruno P Mmbando, Anders Björkman, & Andreas Mårtensson. "Safety of a single low-dose of primaquine in addition to standard artemether-lumefantrine regimen for treatment of acute uncomplicated *Plasmodium falciparum* malaria in Tanzania." Malar J. 2016; 15: 316.

Ngasala, Billy, Irina Jovel, Maja Malmberg, Bruno Mmbando, Anders Björkman, Zul Premji, Andreas Mårtensson, & Richard Mwaiswelo. "Occurrence of day 3 submicroscopic *Plasmodium falciparum* parasitemia before and after implementation of artemether-lumefantrine treatment policy in Tanzania." *PLoS One*. (Submitted).

Ngasala, Billy, Maja Malmberg, Anja M Carlsson, Pedro E Ferreira, Max G Petzold, Daniel Blessborn, Yngve Bergqvist, J Pedro Gil, Zul Premji, & Andreas Mårtensson. "Effectiveness of artemether-lumefantrine provided by community health workers in underfive children with uncomplicated malaria in rural Tanzania: an open label prospective study." Malar J. 2011; 10: 64. Published online 2011 March 16. doi: 10.1186/1475-2875-10-64.

Ngasala, Billy, Maja Malmberg, Anja M Carlsson, Pedro E Ferreira, Max G Petzold, Daniel Blessborn, Yngve Bergqvist, J Pedro Gil, Zul Premji, Anders Björkman, & Andreas Mårtensson. "Efficacy and effectiveness of artemether-lumefantrine after initial and repeated treatment in under five children with acute uncomplicated *Plasmodium falciparum* malaria in rural Tanzania: a randomised trial." *Clinical Infectious Diseases*. 2011 Apr 1;52(7):873-82.

Ngasala, Billy, Marycelina Mubi, Marian Warsame, Max G Petzold, Amos Y Massele, Lars L Gustafsson, Goran Tomson, Zul Premji, & Anders Bjorkman. "Impact of training in clinical and microscopy diagnosis of childhood malaria on antimalarial drug prescription and health outcome at primary health care level in Tanzania: a randomized controlled trial." *Malaria Journal* 2008; 7():199.

Nnko, Elinas J, Charles Kihamia, Filemoni Tenu, Zul Premji, & Eliningaya J Kweka. "Insecticide use pattern and phenotypic susceptibility of Anopheles gambiae sensu lato to commonly used insecticides in Lower Moshi, northern Tanzania." BMC Research Notes 201710:443. https://doi.org/10.1186/s13104-017-2793-4.

Noor, Ramadhani A, Ajibola I Abioye, Anne Marie Darling, Ellen Hertzmark, Said Aboud, Zulfiqarali Premji, Ferdinand M Mugusi, Christopher Duggan, Christopher R Sudfeld, Donna Spiegelman, & Wafaie Fawzi. "Prenatal Zinc and Vitamin A Reduce the Bene t of Iron on Maternal Hematologic and Micronutrient Status at Delivery in Tanzania." *The Journal of Nutrition*. Manuscript received April 11, 2019. Initial review completed May 28, 2019. Revision accepted September 11, 2019. First published online 0, 2019; doi: https://doi.org/10.1093/jn/nxz242.

Ogutu, Bernhards, Alfred B Tiono, Michael Makanga, Zulfiqarali Premji, Adama Dodji Gbadoé, David Ubben, Anne Claire Marrast, & Oumar Gaye. "Treatment of asymptomatic carriers with artemether-lumefantrine: an opportunity to reduce the burden of malaria?" *Malaria Journal* 2010, 9:30 doi:10.1186/1475-2875-9-30. ISSN 1475-2875.

Omuse, Geoffrey, Daniel Maina, Jane Mwangi, Caroline Wambua, Kiran Radia, Alice Kanyua, Elizabeth Kagotho, Mariza Hoffman, Peter Ojwang, Zul Premji, Kiyoshi Ichihara, & Rajiv Erasmus. "Complete blood count reference intervals from a healthy adult urban population in Kenya." *PLoS One* 13(6): e0198444. https://doi.org/10.1371/journal. pone.0198444.

Omuse, Geoffrey , Kiyoshi Ichihara, Daniel Maina, Mariza Hoffman, Elizabeth Kagotho, Alice Kanyua, Jane Mwangi, Caroline Wambua, Angela Amayo, Peter Ojwang, Zul Premji, & Rajiv Erasmus. "Determination of reference intervals for common chemistry and immunoassay tests for Kenyan adults based on an internationally harmonized protocol and up-to-date statistical methods." Published: July 9, 2020. https://doi. org/10.1371/journal.pone.0235234.

Pamba, Allan, Naomi D Richardson, Nick Carter, Stephan Duparc, Zul Premji, Alfred B Tiono, & Lucio Luzzatto. "Plenary paper: Clinical spectrum and severity of hemolytic anemia in glucose 6-phosphate dehydrogenase-deficient children receiving dapsone." *BLOOD* 15 November 2012, Vol 120, number 20 doi:10.1182/blood-2012-03-416032, Pre published online September 19, 2012; 2012 120: 4123-4133.

Premji, Z. "Assessment of anti-malarial therapeutic failures." *Africa Malaria Forum.* No 1-Oct.

Premji, Z & JN Minjas. "Anaemia and Malaria: Determination of packed cell volume using the QBC haematocrit nomograph." Diagnostics in Africa May issue.

Premji, Z, C Makwaya, & JN Minjas. "Current clinical efficacy of chloroquine for the treatment of *Plasmodium falciparum* infections in urban Dar es Salaam, United Republic of Tanzania." Bulletin, WHO, vol 77, no.9, 740-745.

Premji Z, D Ocheng, & C Makwaya. "Monitoring anti-malarial efficacy in routine clinical practice in Tanzania." TMJ vol 17, no 2.

Premji, Z, JN Minjas, & CJ Shiff. "Chloroquine resistant *Plasmodium falciparum* in coastal Tanzania. A challenge to the continued strategy of village based chemotherapy for malaria control." *Trop. Med. Parasitol.* 45, 47-48.

Premji, Z, JN Minjas, & CJ Shiff. "Laboratory diagnosis of malaria by village health workers using the rapid manual ParaSight-F-Test." *Transactions of the Royal Society of Tropical Medicine and Hygiene,* 88, 418.

Premji, Z, P Lubega, Y Hamisi, E Mchopa, JN Minjas, W Checkley, & CJ Shiff. "Changes in malaria associated morbidity in children using Insecticide Treated Bednets in Bagamoyo District of coastal Tanzania." *Trop. Med. Parasitol.* 46, 147-153.

Premji, Z, P Ndayanga, C Shiff, J Minjas, P Lubega, & J MacLeod. "Community based studies on childhood mortality in a malaria holoendemic area on the Tanzanian coast." *Acta Tropica,* 63, 101-109.

Premji, Z, Y Hamisi, C Shiff, JN Minjas, P Lubega, C Makwaya. "Anaemia and *Plasmodium falciparum* infections among young children in an holoendemic area, Bagamoyo, Tanzania." *Acta Tropica,* 59, 55-64.

Premji, Zul. "The malaria enigma in Tanzania: Perceptives and the way forward." *The Dar Graduate,* Vol 4,5,6 N0 1 June 2005.

Premji, Zul, Rich E Umeh, Seth Owusu-Agyei, Fabian Esamai, Emmanuel U Ezedinachi, Stephen Oguche, Steffen Borrmann, Akintunde Sowunmi, Stephan Duparc, Paula L Kirby, Allan Pamba, Lynda Kellam, Robert Guiguemdé, Brian Greenwood, Stephen A Ward, & Peter A Winstanley. "Chlorproguanil-dapsone-artesunate versus Artemether-lumefantrine: a Randomized, Double-blind Phase III

Trial in African Children and Adolescents with Uncomplicated *Plasmodium falciparum* Malaria." *PLoS One*, August 2009 vol 4, issue 8, e6682.

Premji, Zulfiqarali G. "Coartem®: the journey to the clinic." *Malaria Journal* 2009, 8 (Suppl 1): S3 (12 October 2009).

Premji, Zulfiqarali G, Salim Abdulla, Bernhards Ogutu, Alice Ndong, Catherine O Falade, Issaka Sagara, Nathan Mulure, Obiyo Nwaiwuand, & Gilbert Kokwaro. "The content of African diets is adequate to achieve optimal efficacy with fixed-dose artemether-lumefantrine: a review of the evidence." *Malaria Journal* 2008, 7:244doi:10.1186/1475-2875-7-244.

Sattler, Michael A, Deo Mtasiwa, Michael Kiama, Zul Premji, Marcel Tanner, Gerry F Killeen, & Christian Lengeler. "Habitat characterization and spatial distribution of Anopheles sp. mosquito larvae in Dar es Salaam (Tanzania) during an extended dry period." *Malaria Journal*, 2005, 4:4-www.malariajournal.com/content/4/1/.

Saulo, Eleonor C, Birger C Forsberg, Zul Premji, Scott M Montgomery, & Björkman Anders. "Willingness and ability to pay for artemisinin-based combination therapy in rural Tanzania." *Malaria Journal* 2008; 7():227.

Schneider, Achim G, Zulfikar Premji, Ingrid Felger, Tom Smith, Salim Abdulla, Hans-Peter Beck, & Hassan Mshinda. "A point mutation in codon 76 *pfcrt* of *P falciparum* is positively selected for by Chloroquinine treatment in Tanzania." *Infection, Genetics and Evolution*, 1, (2002) 183-189.

Shiff, CJ, W Checkley, P Winch, Z Premji, JN Minjas, & P Lubega. "Changes in weight gain and anaemia attributable to malaria in Tanzanian children living under holoendemic conditions." *Transactions of the Royal Society of Tropical Medicine and Hygiene*, 90, 262-265.

Shiff, CJ, Z Premji, & JN Minjas. "Insecticide Treated Bednets in control of malaria in Africa." *Lancet*, 345: 1375-1376.

Shiff, CJ, JN Minjas, & Z Premji. "The ParaSight-F-Test: A Simple Rapid Manual Dipstick Test to Detect *Plasmodium falciparum* Infection." *Parasitology Today*, vol 10, 12, 494-495.

Shiff, CJ, Z Premji, & JN Minjas. "The rapid manual ParaSight-F-Test. A new diagnostic tool for *Plasmodium falciparum* infection." *Transactions of the Royal Society of Tropical Medicine and Hygiene*, 87, 646-648.

Simba, Daudi O, Deodatus Kakoko, Goran Tomson, Zul Premji, Max Petzold, Margarita Mahindiand, & Lars L Gustafsson. "Adherence to artemether/lumefantrine treatment in children under real-life situations in rural Tanzania." *Transactions of the Royal Society of Tropical Medicine and Hygiene*.

Simba, Daudi O, Deodatus Kakoko, Marian Warsame, Zul Premji, Melba F Gomes, Goran Tomson, & Eva Johansson. "Understanding caretakers' dilemma in deciding whether or not to adhere with referral advice after pre-referral treatment with rectal artesunate." *Malaria Journal*, May 12;9:123.

Simba, Daudi O, Marian Warsame, Deodatus Kakoko, Zakayo Mrango, Goran Tomson, Zul Premjiand, & Max Petzold. "Who Gets Prompt Access to Artemisinin-Based

Combination Therapy? A Prospective Community-Based Study in Children from Rural Kilosa, Tanzania." *PLoS One* 5(8): e12104. doi:10.1371/journal.pone.0012104.

Simba, Daudi O, Marian Warsame, Omari Kimbute, Deodatus Kakoko, Max Petzold, Goran Tomson, Zul Premji, & Melba Gomes. "Factors influencing adherence to referral advice following pre-referral treatment with artesunate suppositories in children in rural Tanzania." *Trop Med Int Health 14:775-83*. Epub 2009 May 26.

Sisowath, Christin, Ines Petersen, M Isabel Veiga, Andreas Mårtensson, Zul Premji, Anders Björkman, David A Fidock, & José P Gil. "In Vivo Selection of *Plasmodium falciparum* Parasites Carrying the Chloroquine-Susceptible *pfcrt* K76 Allele after Treatment with Artemether-Lumefantrine in Africa." *Journal of Infectious Diseases*, 199: 750-7.

Temu, EA, JN Minjas, Z Premji, RH Hunt, & CJ Shiff CJ. "The use of permethrin-impregnated bednets for malaria control in coastal Tanzania: preliminary entomological impact on vectors." *African Entomology*, 7, 233-242.

Whitty, Christopher JM, Richard Allan, Virginia Wiseman, Sam Ochola, Maria Veronicah Nakyanzi-Mugisha, Benjamin Vonhm, Mahemba Mwita, Constantin Miaka, Aggrey Oloo, Zul Premji, Craig Burgess, & Theonest K Mutabingwa. "Averting a malaria disaster in Africa—where does the buck stop." *Bull World Health Organ*, May; 82 (5):381-4.

Winch, PJ, AM Makemba, SR Kamazima, M Lurie, GK Lwihula, Z Premji, JN Minjas, & CJ Shiff. "Local terminology for febrile illnesses in Bagamoyo District, Tanzania and its impact on the design of a community based malaria control programme." *Social Science & Medicine*, vol 42, 7: 1057-1067.

Winch, PJ, AM Makemba, VR Makame, MS Mfaume, MC Lynch, Z Premji, JN Minjas, & CJ Shiff. "Social and cultural factors affecting rates of regular retreatment of mosquito nets with insecticide in Bagamoyo District, Tanzania." *Tropical Medicine & International Health*, 2, 760-770.

Zinc Against Plasmodium Study Group. "Effect of zinc on the treatment of *Plasmodium falciparum* malaria in children: A randomisedcontrolled trial." *The American Journal of Clinical Nutrition*, 76. 805-812.

Appendix 3

Research reports

1. A multicentre, randomised, parallel group study to assess the efficacy, safety and tolerability of a single 400 mg po dose of Oxibendazole suspension versus a single 500 mg po dose of Mebendazole tablet in the treatment of intestinal helminth infections in children.2003, Development Phase III

2. Open label, multicenter study for the evaluation of safety and efficacy of Coartem® (artemether-lumefantrine) tablets (6-dose regimen) in African infants and children in the treatment of acute uncomplicated falciparum malaria. 2003.Clinical Study Report

3. Final report: Social and economic impact of lymphatic filariasis (1995)

4. Final report: Bagamoyo Bed Net Project (1995)

5. Monograph: The implementation and sustainability of Insecticide Treated Mosquito Nets (IMN) programs for malaria control in rural Africa: Lessons learned from the Bagamoyo Bed Net project, Tanzania. (1997)

6. Manual: Acridine Orange method for the laboratory diagnosis of malaria (1998)

7. Final report: Determination and evaluation of willingness to pay for treatment and re-treatment of bed nets as a Malaria control strategy in Bagamoyo District, Tanzania.

8. Final report Community Knowledge, Attitudes and Practices on malaria in Tanzania (1999) Premji Z and Leshabari MT.

9. ZINC – Pemba Project: Technical Report of a WHO-Commissioned Audit Team. April 2004 Prof M. Garenne, Prof A. Prentice, Prof Z Premji

10. Efficacy of co-artemether (artemether-lumefantrine), 6 dose regime, in African infants and children with acute uncomplicated falciparum malaria: Premji Z, Falade CO, Makanga M, Fehintola FA, Adegbola HO, Ogunkunle OO, Falade AG, Ibarra de Palacios P, Stockmeyer M. (Abstract # 36)

11. Co-artemether (artemether-lumefantrine), safety profile of an anti-malarial combination in African infants and children with acute uncomplicated falciparum malaria when treated with the 6 dose-regime: Falade CO, Makanga M, Premji Z, Fehintola FA, Adegbola HO, Ogunkunle OO, Falade AG, Ibarra de Palacios P, Stockmeyer M. (Abstract # 37)

12. Pharmokinetics of the 6 dose-regime of co-artemether (artemether-lumefantrine) in African infants and children with acute uncomplicated falciparum malaria: Makanga M Falade CO, Premji Z, Fehintola FA, Adegbola HO, Ogunkunle OO, Falade AG, Ibarra de Palacios P, Stockmeyer M. (Abstract # 642)

13. A double blind randomised comparison of Chlorproguanil-Dapsone (LapDap) with Sulfadoxine-Pyrimethamine for the treatment of uncomplicated falciparum malaria in young children: A Alloueche, W Bailey, S Barton, J Bwika, P Chimpeni, CO Falade, FA Fehintola, J Horton, S Jaffar, T Kanyok, PG, Kremsner, JG Kublin, T Lang, MA Missinou, C Mkandala, AMJ Oduola, Z Premji, L Robertson, A Sowunmi, SA Ward, PA Winstanley. (Abstract # 789)

Appendix 4

Voluntary Service (in Dar es Salaam)

1. Convener-Sarwar, Aga Khan Welfare Board, 1973 to 1979
2. Member, Ismaili Youth Organization, 1975 to 1979
3. Chairman, Career Guidance Committee, Aga Khan Educational Services,1989
4. Chairman, Jamati Health Committee, Aga Khan Health Services, 1985 to 1990
5. Mukhisaheb, panch baar saal majalis, Darkhana jamatkhana
6. Mukhisaheb, baitul khayal majalis, Darkhana jamatkhana
7. Member without portfolio, Tanzania National Council, 2003

Acknowledgements

In the course of writing this book I have run up many debts of gratitude and it is indeed a pleasure to acknowledge them. In the first place, my sincere thanks to hundreds and perhaps thousands of children who were participants in all the malaria research work that I undertook, which is reflected in this book. To these nameless children goes the credit of my research output, which is today used in malaria diagnosis and treatment.

I wish to acknowledge also my colleagues at Muhimbili University of Health and Allied Sciences, specifically in the Department of Parasitology and Medical Entomology, who were part of my forty years of working life.

I am enormously grateful to my mentors, Professors Minjas, Clive Shiff, Anders Björkman, and Wafai Fawzi.

My PhD students assisted me early on with constructive discussions on the science of malaria; in particular I wish to say a big thank you to my first PhD student Dr Bill Ngasala for all the discourses we had and for unknowingly giving me the confidence to stay on this journey.

To my family I am grateful for encouraging me to embark on this writing project, and my son in particular for reading the first draft and supporting me all the way.

The responsibility for the opinions conveyed in these pages is of course, mine alone. But the opinions themselves were developed, challenged and refined in the course of many conversations with old friends and new acquaintances.

Finally, I would like to thank Mawenzi House Publishers and in particular the editor MG Vassanji for his immeasurable contributions; his professionalism ensured that this book now reaches the reader in such good order.

Zul Premji was born in Iringa, Tanzania, and attended school in two towns before obtaining his medical degree from Muhimbili University of Health and Allied Sciences, Dar es Salaam. He later took an MSc in Medical Parasitology from the London School of Hygiene and Tropical Medicine, a Diploma in Tropical Medicine from the Royal College of Physicians in London, and a doctorate in Infectious Diseases from Karolinska, Sweden. His specialization included clinical trials, antimalarial drug resistance, and malaria case management. Over a career of more than forty years, he has held numerous academic positions in Tanzania, and has been an advisor to National Malaria Control. He now lives in Calgary, Alberta.